# Trauma, Tragedy, Therapy

# Trauma, Tragedy, Therapy

## The Arts and Human Suffering

*Stephen K. Levine*

Foreword by Shaun McNiff

Jessica Kingsley Publishers
London and Philadelphia

First published in 2009
by Jessica Kingsley Publishers
116 Pentonville Road
London N1 9JB, UK
and
400 Market Street, Suite 400
Philadelphia, PA 19106, USA

*www.jkp.com*

Copyright © Stephen K. Levine 2009

**Library of Congress Cataloging in Publication Data**
Levine, Stephen K.
  Trauma, tragedy, therapy : the arts and human suffering / Stephen K. Levine ; fore-
word by Shaun McNiff.
     p. cm.
  ISBN-13: 978-1-84310-512-1 (alk. paper)
  ISBN-10: 1-84310-512-8 (alk. paper)
  1. Arts--Therapeutic use. 2. Psychic trauma. 3. Suffering. I. Title.
  RC489.A72L483 2009
  616.89'1656--dc22

                                                    2009007541

**British Library Cataloguing in Publication Data**
A CIP catalogue record for this book is available from the British Library

ISBN 978 1 84310 512 1

For Paolo Knill: *il miglior fabbro*

*There is nothing stable in the world;*
*uproar's your only music*

— *John Keats*

# Acknowledgments

My thanks to the following journals, in which most of the chapters in this book appeared in their original form: *The Arts in Psychotherapy, POIESIS: A Journal of the Arts and Communication, CREATE: Journal of the Creative and Expressive Arts Therapies Exchange.* Chapter 13, 'Be Like Jacques: *Mimesis* with a *Différance*,' will appear in the volume *Tribute to Derrida*, edited by Avital Ronnell and Wolfgang Schirmacher, Atropos Press, 2009. Chapter 4, 'Trauma, Therapy and the Arts,' first appeared as 'Therapy, Trauma and the Arts,' in *Crossing Boundaries: Explorations in Therapy and the Arts*, edited by Stephen K. Levine, EGS Press, 2002, and in a revised version as 'Tragedy, Trauma and the Art of Time: *Poiesis* in a Dionysian Perspective,' in *POIESIS: A Journal of the Arts and Communication 4*, 2002. The interview by Jean Caron, which formed part of her MA thesis at Lesley University in 1998, was radically rewritten in the light of my current thinking. Almost all the chapters in the current volume have been extensively revised from their original appearance.

I would like to thank my colleagues and students at York University, ISIS-Canada and the European Graduate School, who have stimulated my thinking and continually challenged me to go further, particularly Paul Antze, with whom I have pursued the topic of trauma repeatedly in all these contexts. I owe a special debt to Gabriel Levine, who helped me to find the framework for the book and also edited the manuscript for publication.

# Contents

## Part III: Poiesis *after Post-Modernism*

# Foreword

*Trauma, Tragedy, Therapy* is a bold, brilliant, and imaginative re-visioning of the nature of emotional trauma and its therapeutic treatment. It is a book like no other that I have read in psychology. Stephen K. Levine embraces the darkest elements of experience as the basis of dramatic enactments that transform difficulties into affirmations of human existence. He does nothing less than recast the mission and operation of the whole psychotherapeutic enterprise and the contemporary notions of morality upon which it is based.

As a philosopher, artist, psychologist, therapist, and professor of social science, Stephen K. Levine has spent his life preparing for this book. He is uniquely able to create a text that uses immediate experiences in art and therapy as the basis for a sweeping historical critique of contemporary thought and life. It is a tribute to the expressive arts therapy discipline that our gathering of people from different domains, all committed to caring for the soul and addressing pain and suffering through creative expression, has provided a home for Levine's integrative *poiesis* ('our capacity to shape experience through imagination') over the past two decades.

In this book, Levine takes the relation between trauma and tragedy as his central focus in a presentation that includes other essential themes and issues related to the theory and practice of expressive arts therapy, as well as to his life-long commitment to understanding and furthering human experience through the arts. In addition to his chapters on trauma and the process of *poiesis* as the basis of expressive arts therapy, Levine includes a number of pieces in the form of interviews. Their direct and relaxed dialogical style enables him to state and restate his core positions in a way that complements his more formal writings. The conversational form, paying a certain homage to Plato, enables Levine to convey the legacy of his philosophical influences in colloquial language while modeling one of the book's core ideas – *mimesis*, repeating with variation – in a way that invites readers into the discourse and helps them grasp the conceptual material.

I have been close to Levine's ongoing encounter with the writings of my mentor Rudolf Arnheim (1904–2007), whose predilection toward order challenged Stephen's more improvisational embrace of disarray. I can imagine Rudi smiling at the latest turn in the conversation in which a more complex order is embraced – one that acknowledges creative aspects of chaos and that holds in itself the vital tensions of the world. Levine's succinct presentation of Arnheim's thinking exemplifies the carefully tended seeds of thought and action that are displayed in this volume, gifts to students and to everyone striving to articulate theoretical underpinnings for the practice of expressive arts therapy.

Among the many concerns that Levine addresses is the damage done by the human tendency to adopt stock methods and superficial explanations for the depths, complexities, wonders, and exasperations of human experience, as exemplified so convincingly here by much of current trauma theory. He challenges students to avoid simplistic formulas and to dig deeper when exploring their own work. It is my hope that future generations will take this individuation of thought, art, and social action, as integrated through one person's life, to heart, and that they will sustain the ideal of what the poet Charles Olson, echoing Heidegger, called:

> a man, carved
> out of himself, so wrought he
> fills his given space, makes
> traceries sufficient to
> others' needs
> *(Olson 2001, p.108)*

Contemporary trauma psychology and therapeutic methods have given Stephen K. Levine the material out of which he makes what may be considered his own most defining 'act of *poiesis*,' realizing his dictum of reshaping the world as it is given to us, with all the wounds and suffering we have experienced, and 'making them new.'

By engaging the Holocaust as the defining trauma of his lifetime, Levine cannot be accused of avoiding pain, evil, and wrong-doing, or of taking a light approach to human suffering. This book does not deny the role of rage and forceful action in responding to harmful human behavior. Levine's revolutionary move, his transformative *poiesis*, is his recasting of our understanding of trauma and of our response to it. His core position is that by expressing the painful and tragic experience, we release its fixity and negative hold on our lives, refusing the temptation to assume the role of the victim. Levine clearly shows how memory operates, never completely and literally replicating the past. The act of repeated recall carries within itself a creative element that we do not necessarily appreciate.

The time is ripe for a major change. We must move from a society of victimization to one of creative action – without in any way denying, lessening, justifying, or accepting real trauma, the damage it inflicts, the outrage felt in response to it, or the fervor to prevent more of the same. Psychology and the practice of therapy might start by working on themselves, a message that is implicit in every page of Levine's book. His critique is direct and forceful:

> Psychotherapy has been traumatized: it shows all the symptoms of the trauma victim, suffering from thoughts that are intrusive, constrictive and that tend to hyper-vigilance. What has produced this condition, oddly enough, is the discourse of trauma itself. This discourse intrudes upon our theory and practice even when we wish to think or act otherwise; it constricts us by rendering other forms of suffering opaque. We are always on the alert for trauma, seeing it behind every symptom, as if they were all traumas in disguise. (p.54)

Although he speaks in a clear and forceful voice about the need of psychotherapy to transform itself, Levine's preferred method is modest and far from the heroic salvation suggested by Nietzsche (who otherwise takes on a deservedly iconic role within this book). 'We make art,' Levine says, 'not to be saved but to be seen.' Being witnessed in the expression of our suffering is another core principle of his approach to art and healing. Thus the role of the therapist is largely one of being present to other people and their expressions, furthering a notion of beauty where an experience can 'show itself as it is in itself.'

Those of us who have lived through this era in which all ills tend to be reduced to some form of past trauma and victimization have seen how psychotherapeutic culture and training programs have almost universally supported this trend. Future therapists undergo prescribed training based upon various forms of victimized identity. This is the most recent manifestation of one-dimensional psychological reductionism, replacing and slightly modifying earlier tendencies to attribute emotional difficulties to sexual trauma originating in childhood. The recent era of psychological victimization and identity grievances has achieved an uncanny confluence of moralizing and puritan fundamentalisms on both the left and the right.

Stephen K. Levine's achievement in compassionately turning the tables on trauma psychology can be likened to a startling dream that vividly dramatizes the life we are living and do not see, a 'big dream' that carries a whole complex constellation of emotions and social beliefs. Whether the upheaval of his vision is liberating or disturbing depends on the nature of one's relationship to the prevailing tenets of psychotherapeutic culture of the past two decades.

The process of *poiesis* and the Dionysian forces that inspire Levine call for us to accept the dying of old forms and the loss of soul as prerequisites of renewal. From the ancients we know that things must die in order to be made anew. But the fear of letting go and the unwillingness to be defined in a new way by unexpected and unplanned arrivals is perhaps the core factor that moves people to resist creative expression.

It is quite natural to guard against the crucible of transformation. Human nature tends to flee from encounters with vulnerability and the discomfort of uncertainty. Better to see oneself as a victim, banding together with others in an ever-increasing circle with no limits on the horizon; as Levine says, even the perpetrators are themselves now ultimately seen as victims of abuse. This resistance to creating life anew, to letting go of even the worst things (which play the perverse purpose of maintaining an identity that has a certain usefulness), is so deeply lodged in human experience that it is no wonder that victimization and its accompanying fixations are preferred to creation. Better to hold onto the affliction that defines us than welcome the unknown, and thus possibly lose control over identity. It is not surprising that psychology and therapy are often captured by ideas and social movements that demand less from people, and package reality into trends.

Over my four decades of experience in expressive arts therapy I have learned to welcome these obstacles and sometimes irritating conventions. I have come to see them as my subject matter, the problems that inspire me and help others create. Bad things can be put to good use; as Stephen K. Levine says, 'Chaos is the mother of all beings.' The disturbance we do not want to face can be a source of creative liberation. It is not the easiest of paths, but the way of creation, of *poiesis*, is the one that survives through the millennia as the most reliable cure for the soul.

*Shaun McNiff*
*University Professor*
*Lesley University, Cambridge, MA*

# 1

# Introduction

When I was a child, I would lie in bed at night imagining that I could go back in history to assassinate Hitler. I had no trouble traveling through time, but whenever I tried to carry out my plot, something intervened: either Hitler had a double or the gun misfired. Somehow I could not imagine changing the past. No matter what I did, I could not alter history.

My parents never mentioned the Holocaust. We lived in a house marked by a traumatic event that could not be spoken of. Its presence could only be detected in a general feeling of anxiety: the world was a dangerous place, something bad might happen, and we had to be careful interacting with the *goyim* – they could not be trusted. At the same time, my mother and father did all they could to eliminate any signs of their ancestry without explicitly denying it: giving up the dietary rules, belonging to a synagogue (now called a 'temple') that seemed more Protestant than Jewish, encouraging their children to adapt to the world of others. My sister had a 'nose job' – plastic surgery to remove any trace of *Yiddishkeit* (Jewishness) – and my mother suggested that I might want one too. She also told me that if I wanted to change my last name when I grew up, she would understand. We all went to exclusive private preparatory schools; in mine, I had to dress for chapel and sing Protestant hymns three times a week (the Jewish kids mumbled whenever the name of Jesus came up).

Some of this behavior can be understood as a response to the then-dominant American ethos. To be ethnically distinct was frowned upon; the ideal at the time was the WASP, the White Anglo-Saxon Protestant who behaved properly and spoke genteelly. (In fact, there seemed to be an equation between 'genteel' and 'gentile.') At the same time, the historical predicament of the Jews exaggerated their need to conform: centuries of anti-Semitism culminating in the unspeakable atrocities of the Holocaust resulted in a sense that to stand out as a Jew was to be in danger. Survival could be obtained only by denying one's identity and blending in.

We all react differently to the circumstances of our origins. My brother, seven years older, tried to follow the path of adaptation. He went, by his own choice, to a military academy for preparatory school, then to business school, the army and finally the business world itself. He married a Protestant woman (whose family had converted from Judaism and become Episcopalians) in a secular ceremony and had his wedding party at the St Regis Hotel in New York – at that time a prestigious and distinctly non-Jewish setting. He dressed in Brooks Brothers suits (the Protestant uniform) and prepared me for university by outfitting me in a similar way. Somehow, in the end, it all went wrong. His business career faltered, his marriages failed and his children were taken away (and ultimately raised as Protestants in deep-South Mississippi). He took to drinking and using drugs and died alone in an apartment in Miami. After his death, his daughters found seven guns in the apartment and rooms filled with old newspapers.

I responded in a different way. As a child, my favorite radio program was *The Shadow*, a daily serial preceded by a deep-voiced announcer intoning, 'Who knows what evil dwells in the hearts of men? The Shadow knows.' I identified with the Shadow and wanted to know the things that were being kept hidden, the painful and horrible events that were never – and perhaps could never be – spoken of. No wonder that I later became obsessed with the Holocaust and devoured the literature and film devoted to it. To me, the horror of the Holocaust revealed the ultimate evil dwelling in the hearts of men; I wanted to know about it and to try to understand it. What was not spoken of became the one thing I had to keep in mind at all times.

This is in part a book about understanding trauma, the shattering event that marks a life. It is also a book about the ways that different people respond to such events, in particular the different ways by which they try to find adequate means to come to terms with what has happened to them and to others, to find ways to understand and to be able to live with the memory of what has occurred. Any book about trauma has also to be a book about memory, about how we live with the pain of the past. At the same time, it has to be about the future; our past changes as we re-imagine it in terms of new possibilities for the life ahead of us. Trauma, memory and imagination are united in our understanding and in our way of being. The way we remember the past and imagine the future affects the way we live in the present. Therefore it is essential for us to understand what has happened and to come to terms with it so as to be able to go on living.

What is the proper way to understand trauma? We have to distinguish between the event itself and the categories we employ to think about it. 'Trauma' is not trauma; the concept is different from the experience. In this book, I critically re-examine the concepts by which contemporary thinking has attempted to understand traumatic experience and its aftermath by seeing what assumptions about human experience underlie them and what is the image of human existence that they imply. I also try to develop new ways of understanding trauma that are more adequate to the experience of shattering and fragmentation which is characteristic of this kind of experience. In doing so, I am led to a different conception of human existence than the one that the dominant tradition has given us.

Many of the prevailing conceptions of trauma in psychology and the social sciences seem to me to be inappropriate for understanding human suffering. Paradoxically, the very concepts by means of which contemporary thinking in the human sciences (especially in psychology) have tried to understand trauma have resulted in making it unintelligible. Consequently, practice based on this kind of thinking prohibits people from making sense of their lives in ways that enable them to live productively.

How can we understand trauma in a meaningful way? It seems to me that trauma cannot be properly grasped in a purely cognitive manner. The experience of fragmentation which traumatic suffering entails resists any approach which assumes that experience can be mastered and known through rational discourse. Such a discourse, which is fundamental for our conception of science, is based on the assumption that the subject is capable of mastering existence through knowledge. Reason thus aims for a totality of understanding in which the elements of a field are connected through their mutual significance. Trauma, on the other hand, fragments experience and prevents any totalization into a whole. In so doing, it robs suffering of its meaning. Trauma doesn't mean anything, it just *is*.

How then can we do justice to trauma? How can we represent this kind of experience without giving it a meaning that would integrate it into a systematic whole and thus rob it of its essential character?

I believe that the experience of trauma demands a new conception of the human being, one that is not based on thinking of humans as subjects capable of the mastery of existence through knowledge. We are powerless before trauma; it overwhelms us and plunges us into chaos. And we cannot master it retrospectively through the kind of knowledge that seeks to give it meaning within the totality of experience.

The premise of this book is that only an artistic approach based on what we might call the 'traumatic imagination' is adequate for comprehending the essence of trauma. Artistic expression has always been a fundamental way in which human beings have tried to discover meaning in their lives. The arts are ways of shaping experience, of finding forms that make sense of life through imaginative transformation. However, the arts themselves have primarily been understood within a perspective that is based on systematic knowledge. Aesthetic theory has comprehended art as providing meaning by showing the harmony and unity that can be found within disparate experiences. In this way, art is imagined as capable of reconciling us with life.

The traumatic imagination, on the other hand, rejects the notion of art as providing meaning in extreme suffering. The Holocaust does not mean anything within a universal pattern of history; nor can it be validated as something that has contributed to our capacity to achieve our goals. Such an attribution of meaning and value verges on the obscene. It robs trauma of its essentially tragic character and turns it into melodrama, a superficial experience that leaves the viewer with a feeling of well-being.

To re-imagine trauma means to find ways of representation that are true to its chaotic and meaningless character. It also means to reject the concept of beauty as the presentation of a harmonious totality and to re-figure it within the horizon of terror. In my view, certain artists, such as Samuel Beckett, have been successful in doing so. They have found new forms for the representation of trauma, forms that call into question the prevailing understanding of both trauma and art.

The traumatic imagination is pre-figured in certain artistic forms of the past as well, especially in that of Greek tragedy. If we can understand trauma within the perspective of tragedy, we will see that far from eliminating the pity and the terror of experience, tragedy helps us purify them of their sentimental degradation and face them full on. Tragedy employs what has been called a 'Dionysiac poetics' (Segal 1997), an artistic form that is based on the experience of fragmentation characteristic of the mythical depiction of a god whose essence is to be torn apart and scattered, as seeds are sown in the springtime before their fruits can be gathered in the fall.

The traumatic imagination is also at work spontaneously in the art of those who suffer from mental disorders. So-called 'outsider art,' even when it is appropriated by the dominant discourse of the art world, challenges the aesthetic canon. Its chaotic disorder suits the experience of those who make it and shows us that Dionysian *poiesis* is alive on a naive as well as a sophisticated level.

The arts therapies themselves must be re-imagined in order to make room for this kind of work. We need a therapy of the imagination, one that respects it not as a means toward cognitive understanding but as valuable in its own right. In order to do so, art therapy must be based on a new conception of aesthetics, one in which the traumatic imagination is at the center. One goal of this book is to provide a framework in which to situate a therapy based on the arts. My contention is that in order to do so, we must also re-imagine both art and therapy in ways that take account of the fragmentation that trauma brings. We need to understand the workings of the traumatic imagination and the Dionysian forms to which it gives rise. A meaningful conception of trauma must make room for the imagination; otherwise, we will remain stuck in the past. The imagination takes us forward into the future. If it is rooted in what has actually happened and is not pure fantasy, the imagination can find new artistic forms to represent human suffering.

Not all art is about trauma and human suffering by any means; the arts celebrate the joy that life brings as much as they mourn the losses that mark it. Celebration and mourning are both part of human existence; they have found expression in song, dance, drama, visual art and poetry since human beings have existed on this earth. *Poiesis*, the capacity to shape our experience through the imagination, must take account of both dimensions of our lives. In this book, however, I will focus on the ways in which the arts can come to terms with human suffering. What is the art of trauma? Is *poiesis* capable of responding adequately to suffering? What forms must it develop to do so? Can trauma be represented? In what way? All experience resists representation, trauma perhaps most of all. How can we possibly find a way to represent the unrepresentable, to place an experience that overwhelms us into a delimited form? How, above all, to transform terror into beauty, since all art strives after beauty? What we need is a new way of thinking about trauma that incorporates the imagination, moving away from the view of trauma as the pure repetition of the past. We need to re-imagine trauma in order to understand the role that the imagination plays in the experience of human suffering. In order to do so, we must deconstruct 'trauma' to see how the concept blocks imagination and artistic transformation. But we cannot stop there – we must also look at successful ways of shaping traumatic experience imaginatively. We must study the art of trauma. And we must, as well, look at those modes of practice, both psychological and artistic, that bring an imaginative perspective to bear. We must not only criticize the past; we must also look forward to a possible future.

In a way, this book is an impossible project. It attempts to speak about the unspeakable, and so must necessarily fail in this attempt. Suffering cannot be mastered through understanding; nor, for that matter, can joy. But awareness of our ultimate inability to subject existence to thought does not relieve us of the obligation to think, to attempt to come as close as we can to understanding our experience. Failure to do so means that we will continue to think in unexamined ways, limiting our practice and perhaps even harming those we hope to help.

The book is an essay – in the sense of an attempt, a trial. It is not a scholarly work that tries to do justice to the vast literature on trauma today. Nor is the book a work based primarily on clinical practice. Rather it is a philosophical attempt to think about that which defies understanding.

The kind of thinking which the comprehension of trauma requires must itself incorporate the experience of chaos and fragmentation. It cannot therefore take the form of a system of knowledge but rather must consist of a series of inquiries linked by an underlying concern, inquiries that proceed circuitously along different pathways but nevertheless attempt to arrive at the same destination. The disparate writings contained herein are focused on certain key concepts that recur again and again in different contexts, particularly the concepts of *poiesis* (making, especially art-making) and *mimesis* (imitation or representation). This repetition is apropos: trauma repeats itself, and a discourse that attempts to come to terms with trauma will have to find a form of representation in which repetition can coincide with difference. Such a form can be found only in the poetic (or 'poietic') shaping that can encompass the chaos and fragmentation of traumatic experience without promising any harmonious overcoming of contradiction. To understand this kind of *poiesis* requires a new conception not only of aesthetics but also of human existence itself. If I have not succeeded in this goal, I hope at least to have been 'on the way' to it.

Finally, I hope that readers will find this kind of thinking challenging enough to motivate them to engage in a similar quest for understanding, a quest which can, perhaps, give rise to new forms of imaginative practice, both therapeutic and artistic, that are adequate to our experience of the suffering which is part of human life.

Part I

# From Trauma to Tragedy

# 2

# Going to the Ground

## Reflections on the Foundations of Expressive Arts Therapy

The reflections that follow, first written in the form of journal entries over a number of years, attempt to probe the philosophical foundations of the arts therapies, the basic concepts and principles that underlie the practice of a field which claims that art can be an adequate response to suffering. The writing points to the fact that ultimately the ground of our work is not psychology, the theoretical understanding of the mind, but *poiesis*, the human capacity to respond to and change the world through the act of shaping what is given to us. I have kept the entries close to their original form, in order to give the reader the sense of a thinking in process of development, struggling with ideas, trying to reach its own ground.

## ON THE FOUNDATIONS OF EXPRESSIVE ARTS THERAPY

We often talk about having a phenomenological basis for our field. What is a phenomenon? That which shows itself to us. What is our proper relation to it? To pay attention. If we pay careful attention, it will reveal itself.

> 'Attention is the natural prayer of the soul.' – Malebranche (Lacoue-Labarthe 1999, p.64)

How can we speak about the phenomenon? How can we say what shows itself, name it, point it out, describe it, tell it? We need to let the phenomenon speak, help it to name itself, to tell its story. But perhaps there is more than one story? Perhaps there are multiple stories, many discourses and dialogues. This is what Lyotard (1984) means when he says that there are no more 'master narratives,' that we can no longer believe in the existence of one true story that contains the whole, as the Bible once did for many in the West.

There are different ways of telling stories; one of them is through *poiesis*, making or shaping. We know something by shaping it, by giving it a form. Art-making is a way of shaping the truth, of 'setting it into a work' (Heidegger 1975, p.39). In so doing, we let the truth of what the work points to show itself. When it does, we have the experience of beauty.

Beauty is the phenomenon *par excellence*. It is what happens when we are able to let that which we experience show itself as it is in itself. This explains the power of the arts in our lives as well as in the therapeutic space. The proper response to such a showing would be awe. Heidegger (1949, p.391) also tells us, 'The poet names what is holy.' In the face of the holy, what can we feel but awe?

It is the faith of our therapeutic work that this beauty can be found in chaos as well as in order, in suffering as well as in joy. How can we understand this? In therapy what shows itself is what we can call the 'soul' of the person. 'Soul' refers to what enables that person to come alive, to be the particular being that they are. Psychotherapy, then, is an attending to the showing of the psyche or soul. James Hillman (1975, pp.50–51) seems to say something like this when he speaks of the goal of therapy as 'soul-making.' I understand this to mean a kind of shaping in which the beauty of the person comes to stand forth and shine. How does it do this? Through the image. Soul shows itself through images, through the imagination. That is why Hillman (1970) distinguishes between the 'language of psychology and the speech of the soul,' a phrase I have myself appropriated as the subtitle of an earlier book (Levine 1997).

Psychology articulates itself in concepts, but the psyche needs the image in order to come forth, whatever form the image may come to take, whether in pictures, words, sounds, movements or scenes. The image allows the psyche to reveal itself in ways that transcend the order produced by rational discourse. One of these ways is through the manifestation of suffering; the most chaotic parts of the psyche can be grasped only by means of the imagination, not by conceptual thought. The therapist attends to the suffering of the soul, its psycho-pathology. The therapist attends to its suffering, pays attention to it and helps it to show itself, to present itself, to become present. In so doing, the suffering becomes a present, a gift to be treasured. This is hard to hold onto; we want to eliminate the pain, but perhaps the pain is part of the gift – if we could find a way to hold it, a way to be with it and not run away from it.

We show ourselves most clearly when we are in crisis, when everything else falls away. Karl Jaspers (1995, p.40) talks about the boundary-situation (*Grenzsituation*), the point at which we are at our limits and have no recourse. It is, he says, an experience of shipwreck, in which we have lost our anchor and gone aground. What would it mean to heal in such a situation? Perhaps healing is also a mode of being present, of attending to the suffering, of letting it find its form. The arts give a form to the suffering of the soul, a ritual communal structure in which it can be held. I think of songs of mourning – and of praise, for surely we show ourselves in joy as much as in pain. How can we think praise and loss, joy and sorrow, together? The Hebrew prayer for the dead, the *Kaddish*, is a praise of God's glory in the face of death. Could this be a model for our work?

## ON ART AND KNOWLEDGE

In classical Greek culture, the arts were the principal means by which education was carried out. The mytho-poetic tradition on which the culture rested was carried by the words of the poets, especially Homer. This began to change when philosophy came upon the scene. Socrates sought for a logical ground for tradition; by challenging the commonly held beliefs through argument and disputation, he also laid the groundwork for a challenge to the arts in which these beliefs were embodied. Plato drew the logical conclusion to this approach in *The Republic*, when he suggested that in the ideal city, built upon knowledge and not belief, the poets would not be admitted. Thus he resolved what he called 'the ancient quarrel between poetry and philosophy' by exiling the poets from the *polis*, from the space of public life.

From then on, the arts were considered to have nothing to do with knowledge; art and science became strangers to one another. It was not until Nietzsche that this separation was radically challenged. Nietzsche tried to restore the primacy of the arts; for him *poiesis* gave access to a truth denied to logical thought. Logic depends on the principle of contradiction; but what if existence is contradictory at its core? Nietzsche saw the contradictory nature of Being as consisting in its temporality. If there is no ideal world of eternal truth, then both religion and science can be viewed as myths which keep us from the abyss that is at the heart of things. Only by looking into this abyss could we find the truth. 'One must have chaos in one, to give birth to a dancing star,' Nietzsche said (2003, p.46). I would prefer to say, 'One must have chaos in one, to give birth to a dancing god.' The dancing god would be Dionysos, who embodies the image of Nature ever changing, coming into being and passing away, bringing both life and death. For Nietzsche, only the tragic poet, not the philosopher, can look into the abyss and say, 'Yes!' Can we who live in times that have seen such horror make this affirmation today?

Martin Heidegger has tried to carry Nietzsche's thought further. If the essence of existence is time (as he tells us), then our own being is marked by this passing, especially by the end that awaits us all. Death breaks up all our attempts to find a solid ground on which to stand; for Heidegger, it is only in facing our mortality resolutely that we can find an authentic way to live, a way which is truly our own.

The tone of Heidegger's early work has an heroic cast to it – the solitary individual who faces death, an enemy greater than he is, and who is willing to do battle with it. Heidegger's critique of the inauthenticity of everyday life resonated at the time with the ideology of National Socialism, which promised a glorious future for a Germany that could live without Christian piety or bourgeois distractions. It is not clear whether the ideas of *Being and Time* (1962) are opposed to Nazism or lead in its direction (or both), but, without justifying him, one can see how Heidegger was tempted to take that path.

We know that he ultimately withdrew from politics and was forbidden to teach by the Nazi regime, that he went into solitude in the Black Forest and devoted his time to writing essays about, among other things, the relationship between poetry and thought, and that the arts, especially the poetry of Hölderlin, became his central preoccupation. Was this 'turn' in his thinking a repudiation of his earlier work or a development of it? The question is a burning one, since Heidegger remains the central figure in the post-modern tradition, the thinker for whom poetry became a primary path to truth. How can we accept that a Nazi could play such a role? Or to put it another way, if the Holocaust is the antithesis of *poiesis*, then how is it possible to think them together?

## THESES CONCERNING *POIESIS* AS THE GROUND OF EXPRESSIVE ARTS THERAPY

The fundamental problem for thinking is the problem of the foundation. What is the ground of our thought? Philosophy criticizes belief or common opinion in order to find a ground on which to stand. This ground cannot be proven; we can prove only theorems that are derived from axioms themselves set forth or posited. The ground, then, is something that I stake out – here I stand, as Luther said, here I make my claim.

We think today in the shadow of post-modernism. In spite of all claims to the contrary, we have not left post-modernism behind, since the historical situation that gave rise to it has not been left behind. The situation is one in which we are no longer confident of having a ground for our beliefs. Post-modernist philosophy is thus based on a critique of foundationalism, the idea that there is something that can act as a fundamental basis for thought. As a consequence, post-modernism becomes a critique of philosophy itself, in so far as the latter seeks for a ground. Moreover, post-modernism sees a connection between foundationalism and fundamentalism – fundamentalism asserts its foundation as given, whether by God or in some other way.

Instead of a foundation, post-modernism introduces the idea of story. The ground that we posit is a fiction, something made or made up; in other words, a product of *poiesis*. We tell stories about our lives; we make narratives that give our lives meaning. However, there is no one story, no master narrative. Rather each story relates a particular way of life, a practice or *praxis*. The multiplicity of stories constitutes our world.

If each practice has a story as its ground, on what story is the practice of expressive arts therapy grounded? Its ground, I would maintain, is not to be found in theory, *theoria*, but in making, *poiesis*. However, it seems to me that the traditional concept of *poiesis* does not offer us any ground on which to stand. Therefore it has to be 'deconstructed,' taken apart in order to explore its underlying assumptions. For Plato, *poiesis* is *mimesis* or imitation. The artist imitates what he sees and thus is removed from what is real. Even what is 'real,' for Plato, the world in which we live, is only an imitation of the ideal form of things, the eternal and unchanging paradigm that the world itself imitates. The artist is thus thrice removed from truth, which would consist of the direct intuition of an eternal form or idea.

For Aristotle, on the other hand, form can be embodied; the idea or form can be realized in matter. That is why Aristotle grants a cognitive value to *poiesis*. Although not theory, not the pure contemplation of ideal form in itself, *poiesis* is a kind of knowing, a knowing by making. The artist must have an idea of the form that is to be realized; he then works on the material to help it embody the form. We know the work in so far as we recognize the form. *Poiesis* is still a kind of *mimesis* for Aristotle, though now the form to be imitated is in the mind of the maker and not in an ideal realm of Being.

The tradition of aesthetics is, then, a formalistic one. Beauty is conceived of as the perfection of form. For Kant, who laid the foundations of modern aesthetic philosophy, the proper way to grasp beauty is through disinterested contemplation. The spectator or audience observes the work at a distance. The work is thus detached from the will; it has no purpose, no role in the striving that constitutes our life, though it seems somehow purposeful in its own right. It is, as Kant (1987, p.73) says, a kind of 'purposiveness without a purpose.'

By removing the work of art from the instrumental concerns of everyday life in this way, Kant is able to view it as bringing about a harmony between the different faculties of the mind, between cognition and practice, knowledge and will. Such a harmony symbolizes the reconciliation between the finite and the infinite, the finite world given to us through our senses and the unlimited object of reason. The contact with the infinite that the work brings thus ennobles the mind, elevates it from the tawdriness of our petty concerns and puts us in touch with the eternal. This is why, in the European tradition, the arts are seen as the property of the cultivated person, the one who rises above the business of daily life.

Nietzsche, however, breaks this tradition of thinking. For him, the power of the arts lies not in their taking us out of our changing world into a higher plane, a perfect existence in which temporality and mortality are overcome, but rather in their ability to plunge us directly into the heart of things, into the chaos of incessant striving, of the thrust of time which beats ever onward, breaking down what has been and building up what will come. Nietzsche's break with the philosophical tradition, with its emphasis on form and intellect, can be said to represent the birth of post-modernism, a mode of thinking which attempts to understand the temporal character of existence as something that is ineluctable and cannot be overcome.

By prioritizing temporality and change, post-modernism challenges
the very basis of philosophy, which has always aimed at the eternal and
unchanging. A consequence of this challenge is that the conceptual and
systematic form of philosophy itself needs to be re-thought. Concepts
aim at consistency; for Descartes, the founder of modern thought,
an idea must be both clear and distinct in order to be accepted as
true. If the changing nature of existence prohibits such consistency,
then conceptual thought itself comes into question. Post-modern
philosophy looks to the image rather than the concept as the primary
access to truth, since only the image can embody contradictions in
this way. *Poiesis*, which operates through the imagination, thus can
be rehabilitated. The ancient quarrel between philosophy and poetry
becomes an alliance based on friendship, in which the thinker honors
the arts as a way towards wisdom. Heidegger completes this destruction
or deconstruction of the aesthetics of the tradition. He reconnects *poiesis*
to both truth and world. In *Being and Time*, truth is understood not in
the Platonic sense of *mimesis*, correspondence to a pre-existing reality,
but as *aletheia*, the remembering or uncovering of what is hidden and
needs to be brought into the open to be seen (Heidegger 1962). The
work then does not 'represent' the world, it does not copy or imitate
what we experience; rather the work wrests the truth of the world from
out of its hiddenness and brings it to appearance. Moreover, this truth is
not an ideal form, the eternal verity hidden behind the veil of changing
appearances. Rather truth is the coming-to-show-itself of the world as
it has been and can be, its actuality and possibility, its temporal and
historical manifestation. *Poiesis*, therefore, does not imitate or represent
what is already there; rather it brings into being what has never been
but what stands revealed as the truth of that which is.

*Poiesis* brings the truth into appearance in the world through
'instituting' it in a work; art is, Heidegger (1975) says, the setting-itself-
into-a-work of truth. In this way, the work 'sets up' a world. The world
is the totality of what shows itself and gives meaning to all the pathways
of our lives. By setting up a world, the work helps us to see for the first
time who we are, and we are changed by this revelation. The work is
a gathering of our life and times into a pattern, a *Gestalt* or structure
that we can recognize. This structure is not to be understood as pure
form, in the traditional sense of something outside of time and change.
Rather it is the particular historical manifestation of our being at this

moment. Suddenly we see ourselves at this moment in time and we are forced to re-vision our conception of who we thought we were.

If the world that is set up by the work is an historical and not an eternal one, then it cannot be made by an imposition of ideal form upon brute matter. Again, the truth of the work is not its form. There is something in the work that resists form, something that cannot be abstracted and made into an object of contemplation, as the tradition envisaged. What holds itself back from appearance is what Heidegger (1975, p.46) calls 'Earth.' The work for him is a struggle between World and Earth, between manifestation and concealment, a struggle which has been brought into a structure in which that struggle itself is revealed. That is why works of art can never be completely understood or reduced to a formula. Something in the work will always remain hidden and will demand continued uncovering.

Moreover, what shows itself will be different at different times. The meaning of a work depends on its reception in a particular historical period. Works of the past need to be made manifest all over again in the light of the world in which we live. Each time invents its own history.

The concept of 'Earth' in Heidegger is necessarily an obscure one, and its very obscurity attests to its relevance. 'Being loves to hide,' said Heraclitus. If this hiddenness is intrinsic to the temporal character of Being, which has no eternal form that could reveal itself to philosophical intuition, then we cannot ever expect to achieve the knowledge that philosophy has always aimed for. We will always see through a glass darkly, for we cannot get outside of time. This does not mean that truth does not exist; rather it requires us to re-think the meaning of truth in a way that is appropriate to mortal beings, to those who must live in time. 'Earth,' therefore, testifies to the hiddenness of truth and can never become a clear and distinct concept.

To be in time means to be embodied. Earth is in the body of the work, its sensuous manifestation, the colors and shapes of the painting, the sounds and rhythms of the words. That is why a reproduction cannot show a painting properly and why translation always fails the poem. Through its embodiment of the struggle between World and Earth, the work of art shows us the truth of sensible experience, the very thing that philosophy in its quest for the eternal has claimed to be impossible.

Just as the work demonstrates the limits of our knowledge, it also shows the boundaries of our will. If there is no ideal form which we can impose upon matter by our will, from whence, then, does the work come? Heidegger's radical solution stems from his basic idea: we are in the world as mortal beings enmeshed in time; we cannot therefore master this world. Such a position of mastery would require that we stand outside the world, as God is thought to do. Rather the world comes to us; it is given to us in our history. Our task is to enable it to show the possibilities that are hidden in what is past. Thus the work arises not from mastery but from an attitude of openness to what is given, a receptivity that lets the world be what it can be. This attitude of *Gelassenheit* or 'letting-be' is not a mode of passivity. Passivity makes sense only as the opposite of mastery. Letting-be means openness to what is coming, to the event of manifestation (*Ereignis*) that we welcome into the world. The artist is not the master, the god-like imposer of form upon chaos, he is the one to whom the work comes, who humbly opens himself to its arrival in the world.

Beauty, then, is the appearance of truth in sensible form. The work gives us the presentation of truth as that which presents itself. In that sense, art is, as Jean-Luc Nancy (1996, p.34) says, the presentation of presentation. The sensible manifestation of truth is therefore not a defect but its highest possibility. 'O taste and see,' says the psalmist; the truth is made present to our senses and thus makes sense. Beauty strikes us in our bodies; it takes our breath away; it moves or touches us; we are stirred by it. The experience of beauty is not an act of disinterested contemplation but one of being shaken to the core of our being, an experience so strong that it tells us, as Rilke's poem does, 'You must change your life' (Rilke 1984a, p.61).

The artist is thus the attendant of beauty, not the master of it. If she can become open, then something may come to her; something may be given which can be responded to by a further act of shaping. Even at that point, the artist cannot shape the work by an act of will but must submit to its dictates, and discover what it needs to be manifest. Michelangelo's notion that the sculptor frees the work from the block of stone in which it is hidden comes closest to capturing this understanding of the relationship between artist, work and material.

The same attitude is present, I believe, in therapeutic practice. In that sense all therapy can be considered as an act of *poiesis*. Not that the therapist can make the client well, but that she can help allow the truth of the client's existence to emerge, a truth which can give meaning and purpose to the client's life. The therapist is thus a facilitator and a witness to what can arrive.

Traditional philosophical aesthetics cannot therefore serve as a theoretical foundation for expressive arts therapy; we need a new conception of art-making founded on a different *Menschenbild*, a different image of what it means to be human. In such a conception, *theoria* would not be the primary human characteristic, as it is, for example, in Aristotle's description of the human being as the 'rational animal.'

Rather, what is primary is the kind of knowing which comes before reflection. This is a tacit knowledge that can be said to be the intelligence of the senses. Merleau-Ponty's (2002) notion of the 'lived body' (*le corps vécu*) expresses this insight. We are in the world as embodied beings, and our body has an understanding of the world that we are in. Sensing is also making sense. Theory, or reflective knowledge, is founded upon this primary inherence in the world through the senses.

We need a thinking that is friendly to the arts, a poetic/meditative thinking, if we are to think in a way that is appropriate to our work. What form would this thinking have to take?

## ON DECENTERING AND EXPRESSIVE ARTS THERAPY

One of the difficulties that the tradition of philosophy engenders is that it looks for a center of thought, a unifying concept that would control all others. Traditional thinking places the truth at the center. The center is then distinguished from the margin, that which lies outside of truth, goodness and beauty. These qualities are reserved for 'civilized' peoples, that is, those who live in the great civilizations, particularly Europe, which is taken to possess its highest form. Thus the philosophical concept of a unifying center is ultimately a political concept.

In our post-colonial world, however, we can no longer accept such a distinction between center and margin, between Europe and other civilized nations on the one hand (primarily those that have been settled by Europeans or that have accepted European guidelines) and the rest of the world on the other ('primitive' or 'Eastern' cultures). Rather, in the words of the poet W.B. Yeats (2000, p.154), 'the centre cannot hold.' Eurocentrism can no longer be unthinkingly accepted, nor can the conception of the arts which it implies. In this conception, the arts are regarded as 'fine' or 'high,' rarefied objects to behold at a distance from everyday life, from the body and from the purposeful round of activities in which we normally engage. The artist himself is a special being, possessed of 'genius,' a capacity not available to ordinary people. And the arts are similarly set aside, reserved for special places, the museum, the concert hall, the theater, to be regarded in a quiet and reverential manner by those whose sensibilities have been cultivated to an adequate degree. Everything else is entertainment, popular or folk art, to be enjoyed by the 'lower' classes, those without the cultivation and manners necessary for the appreciation of the finer things in life.

Here, as elsewhere, we can see that to be at the center also means to be superior – in wealth, education, breeding and status. The concept of 'fine art' as a political concept is ultimately rooted in imperial conquest and in a framework of thinking in which the ideal is privileged over the real – in which being, conceived as perfection and eternity, has priority over becoming, the flux of the sensible world in which things come into existence and pass away.

It is important, however, not to fall into the trap of a simple reversal of values, to valorize only what is 'uncivilized,' what is 'outside,' 'marginal,' or 'primitive.' The great works of European culture (like the great works of other imperial civilizations) are magnificent achievements. The mistake of political and artistic movements which attempt to formulate an identity between the arts and everyday life is repeated by counter-cultures which aim to return to an idealized simplicity and primitivism which in fact never existed in historical reality.

Civilization begins with literacy. It is true that oral cultures integrated the arts into everyday life to a greater extent. Artistic expression was available to everyone in some way, and the arts had a sensuous immediacy that is sometimes missing from the traditional practice of the fine arts as we know it. In this way the arts (song, dance, story) as well as artists (singers, dancers, story-tellers) were integrated into the daily round of work activities to a much greater degree than in complex civilizations.

Nevertheless the arts, as ways in which life is presented rather than lived, have always been set aside, or 'sacred,' in the original meaning of the word, recognized as different from everyday purposeful work activities. This separation was understood by 'primitive' peoples as well. The Trobriand Islanders told Malinowski that without the proper ritual carvings and prayers, their canoes would sink. At the same time, they made it clear that if the canoes were not made properly, they would sink as well (Malinowski 1984).

There is a necessary distinction between art and life, between activities that are purely instrumental and those that are primarily presentational. However, in the modern conception of the fine arts, this distinction has been widened into a complete separation, even to the extent, in high modernism, of wishing to banish from art everything that reminds us of the everyday (the figure in painting, story in dance, melody in music, and so on). The tension between art and life will always remain. This is not a defect but the very power of the arts, that they step aside a moment and show us the fullness of life in which we are normally immersed. For a moment, we can stop and give our attention to the work, we can 'wonder,' in the sense in which Aristotle saw that experience as the origin of philosophy. The attempt to overcome the distance between art and life results in a loss of the aesthetic experience. It is as one-sided as the tendency in the aesthetics of fine art to make that distance absolute.

The notion that we must choose between a fine art in which there is no connection to everyday life and a popular art in which they are identical is itself grounded in the conception of center and margin which expressed the political domination of the great civilizations over the rest of the world. As long as this conception is maintained, we can choose only between a fine art divorced from life and a popular art in which there is no separation at all. What would it be like to ground our thinking in a different way than in terms of the relation between center and margins? What would it be like to think in a decentered way? How would that affect our understanding of the arts?

Such a way of thinking is demanded by our changed historical reality. We no longer live in a world in which one civilization dominates the rest or, at least, we no longer take such domination as natural. Today there is no political center, and as a result no one canon for artistic expression. In the contemporary world, the creative impulse often comes from what were once the margins, from formerly colonized countries, those that were excluded from positions of power: the dispossessed, the insulted and injured of the world. Victor Turner (1995) saw this clearly in his writings on 'liminality' – those who occupy a liminal space outside of recognized and legitimate positions often carry the creative impulse from which something new can be born. In the United States, for example, Jews and blacks were among the most culturally creative groups after the Second World War. Today new immigrant peoples are beginning to play that role. And 'outsider art,' the art of the unschooled, the insane, the excluded, is moving to the inside as a recognized mode of expression. Of course, this raises the question of how the outsider can keep his authenticity when moving into the center. Does the work not run the risk of being appropriated by the dominant culture, especially by the entertainment industry (witness the fate of hip-hop and rap music)? Some groups embrace this fate; others try to fight it by willfully staying outside. I wonder whether a third possibility is not available: to make something new from the encounter of the margin with the center. This would be an authentic mode of decentering.

Decentering in expressive arts therapy has been proposed by Paolo Knill and Herbert Eberhart as a way of gaining distance from the problem, moving away from the central issue that the client brings (Eberhart 2002; Knill, Levine and Levine 2005). To some extent, this is a question of method; exclusive focus on a problem can lead to a form of circular thinking in which alternatives are excluded. In another sense, however, decentering can be said to constitute the essence of expressive arts therapy, since the arts themselves decenter from everyday life. No matter how close the relationship seems between art and life, they will never be identical; and it is in the difference that separates them that the value of art emerges.

The expressive arts therapist could then be considered as an expert in moving from the center to the margin and returning home, from the literal reality of the world to its imaginal possibilities and back again in order to find a new perspective. This capacity to cross over is grounded in the arts-based orientation of expressive arts, for the artist is always moving back and forth between the real and the possible. If we regard the expressive arts therapist as a cross-over artist, perhaps we can find the proper framework for understanding a practice that is itself often relegated to the margins of the mental health profession.

The marginalization of the expressive and creative arts therapies goes hand in hand with the marginalization of those who suffer the most and whose maladies are the most resistant to cure. Arts therapists are often put in the position of helping the most excluded members of the community, those with severe mental illness, people suffering from autism, dementia and other forms of disability that do not respond to traditional psychotherapy or counseling. And expressive arts therapists are themselves marginalized, relegated to second- or third-hand status in clinics and other institutions, poorly paid and undervalued. Yet it is often the case that a therapy based on the arts is the only one that is effective with the most difficult clients. If we were to regard the expressive arts therapist as someone who can move from the center to the margin and back again, and who can, like Hermes, carry messages from one realm to another, then perhaps we would have a more productive image of the profession than if we were to try to 'normalize' it, that is, to become more clinical, professional and scientific, as we often feel pressured to do. Perhaps we need a decentered conception of the profession of expressive arts therapy in order to take account of the special nature of our field. Then we could stand upon our identity as professionals who can move between different worlds and be comfortable in the spaces between them.

## ON TRAUMA, MEMORY AND THE ARTS

In the literature on trauma, victims are often depicted as passive and helpless. Trauma happens to them, and they receive it or take it in without being able to do anything about it. In fact, this is one of the definitions of trauma: it renders the person to whom it happens helpless.

In some ways, this account corresponds to the experience of trauma. A rape victim, for example, almost always has no control over what happens to her; she is the passive subject of a horrendous experience that she cannot stop or mitigate. To think otherwise would be to blame the victim, to attribute rape, for example, to some action on her part – wearing seductive clothing, walking in a dangerous area of the city, and so on. It is clear that in this sense the victim is in no way responsible for the trauma; not only is provocation a myth, but even were it to occur, she would not be responsible for the act, any more than a victim of a terrorist attack or military assault is responsible for the event, no matter what his country may have done to make such an attack possible. To ascribe agency to the victim of trauma is to deny the trauma itself.

However, there is a sense in which the trauma victim is not purely passive, in so far as his experience of the event is something that is his own and that cannot be denied. This is why every traumatic event is experienced differently by different people. No two experiences are the same, though there may be typical responses. Every account of trauma therefore is specific to that person and must be attended to without remaining fixed in already formulated theoretical categories. Otherwise the victimhood of the person is repeated in the treatment: the therapist or trauma worker is conceived of as acting upon someone who is incapable of shaping the traumatic experience and who can only be affected in some way by others, those whose job it is to help.

One of the problems with trauma theory is that it relies on an implicit conception of the human subject as a being defined by consciousness and will. This conception is the heritage of the tradition of Western thought, which, in its modern form, is to be most clearly found in Descartes. In the Cartesian formulation, 'I think, therefore I am,' the human being is identified with a consciousness that is fully aware of itself and capable of carrying through its projects according to its self-knowledge. Such a conception of what it means to be human also corresponds to the notion of a divine being who is both omniscient and omnipotent. In so far as 'man' is made in God's image, he therefore aspires to this condition of total knowledge and control.

In a sense, the Western archetype of the human is that of the hero, the one who knows his destiny and can act to achieve it. It is an image which fits the imperial nature of Western civilization but which is not specific to it. Perhaps, we might even say, it is the self-image of human experience in general. Whether we ascribe it to evolutionary imperatives (the need to know and control our environment in order to survive), to psychological needs (the narcissistic desire to be recognized as perfect by the other) or to the existential dread of our mortality (the attempt to deny the awareness of our finitude), the conception of the subject as conscious and in control arises from deep-seated human needs.

For that reason, it is not only in the West that this self-concept is dominant; otherwise Eastern thought would not need to emphasize so much the necessity of letting go of the ego to achieve enlightenment. What is specific to our culture is that this conception has been reflectively grasped and thematized as constituting what it means to be human. Consequently we take this concept as given, and unthinkingly base our theoretical frameworks which try to understand human behavior upon it. This is especially true for trauma theory, in which we are attempting to account for an experience in which subjects experience themselves as being without full awareness and control. Within our normal framework, not to exercise the power of the conscious subject is not to have an experience at all. This is the reason why trauma victims are sometimes thought of as not capable of remembering and shaping the traumatizing event. There is no other way for us to understand what has happened to them because we only have one way of understanding experience in general, namely as the experience of conscious, self-aware subjects in control of their acts.

One of the great accomplishments of post-Cartesian thinking, especially within the phenomenological tradition, has been to reflect upon the ground of experience, the ongoing awareness that I do not make into a theme or bring fully to my attention but which is nevertheless mine. We could say it is experience without a subject – that is, without a self-conscious ego accompanying it. Far from being a rare phenomenon, it is what constitutes the overwhelming majority of our experiences, especially in perception. Without being explicitly aware of it, I am constantly undergoing a set of experiences in which what is given to me through the senses is taken in, shaped and brought into a non-totalizing unity. This awareness is accessible to reflection but is not under the control of a conscious 'I.' Husserl (2001) called it the 'passive synthesis' of consciousness; for Sartre (2001) it is 'pre-reflective' awareness; and for Merleau-Ponty (2002), it is the experience of the 'lived body,' a generalized body-awareness that underlies consciousness.

In our experience, sense-making is always going on, even when we are not aware of it. This also means that perception cannot be understood, as it has been within the philosophical tradition for the most part, as the purely passive imprint of an external stimulus upon a sense organ. In so far as sense-making happens, there is an element of shaping in sensing; what is given is received in a specific manner, taken up and made part of an ongoing flow of awareness. Even in perception, therefore, there is what we could regard as a creative element, a shaping which is not done by the conscious ego but which nevertheless takes place. The word for this kind of shaping might be 'receptivity,' a third term between activity and passivity, one that signifies an active passivity, an experience that happens without the ego's knowledge and control. Happening and receptivity are the ground of human experience; the activity of the conscious ego is built upon them and depends on them for its existence, not the other way around.

We must be able to conceive of experience without an ego in order to be able to formulate an adequate theory of trauma and to find appropriate ways to respond to it. In theories of trauma, it is often said that the traumatic event overwhelms the ego; the event is thought of as too great to be encompassed within the ego's boundaries. It is said to 'shatter' the ego. As a consequence, according to this framework, the trauma is not actually experienced. Therefore it cannot be remembered but can recur only in its original form.

This theoretical understanding does do justice to the way in which traumatic experience occurs without the ego's participation; I have no control over it, neither do I have full awareness of it. However, the theory also implies that the trauma is not experienced at all, that there is necessarily a blank in the subject's experience which prohibits memory from taking place. Such a conception would in fact deny the vast majority of experiences that certainly deserve to be considered traumatic, those experiences of suffering in which there is not a sense of conscious control, but in which there is nevertheless a pre-reflective awareness which renders the traumatic event capable of being remembered, even if the victim might wish to push the memory away.

Moreover, not only does this theory not do justice to the capacity of most trauma victims to remember their experience, but also it neglects the way in which even trauma, which interrupts and shatters the experience of the subject, is nevertheless an experience – that is, something shaped by the person, albeit in a receptive, non-active way. This is why the 'same' traumatic event is experienced so differently by different victims. We tend to ascribe an identical experience to every victim of trauma and, in so doing, we rob them of agency all over again. Even in the concentration camps, there were many ways in which the traumatic experience of the horror was taken in and responded to. In each case traumatic experience is already what we might call 'pre-shaped,' that is, received and responded to in a characteristic way.

It does not take away from the experience of the traumatized person to say that no experience is purely passive; on the contrary it restores to them the ground of their existence without ascribing to them any sort of complicity in the act. Moreover it makes it possible to understand how the victim can respond to trauma, how the experience of helplessness can in fact be dealt with in creative ways. In the camps, there were not only those who became what were called 'Muselmen,' automatons seemingly without any human capacity to act (Agamben 1999). There were also those capable of engaging in acts of resistance and of solidarity that denied the Nazi attempt to destroy the souls of the inmates. Such acts would be incomprehensible without a different understanding of what it means to be human than the one that normally underlies the theory of trauma.

Not only is the account of perceptual experience faulty in the prevailing theoretical framework, but also memory does not receive its full due. Memory in that framework is thought of as the passive imprint of prior experiences, but reflection shows that memory is never a pure reproduction of a previous experience (just as that experience itself was not a purely passive one). Memory works on experience, selects and shapes it, even if we have no conscious control over the shaping. Therefore memory, as much as perception, could be said to have a creative component. In fact, all human experience is creative, even when it is not under the guidance of a conscious ego.

This creative ground of human experience is what makes possible artistic creativity, and it is important that we carry our account of the human subject into this realm as well. In the prevailing traditions of aesthetics, the creativity of the artist is understood either as the pure activity of genius or as an absolutely passive state in which 'inspiration' happens to the person without his or her participation. These frameworks seem to account for certain aesthetic phenomena – on the one hand, the way in which an artist can formulate a project and carry it out according to a plan, and on the other hand, the way in which images seem to arrive without anyone anticipating them.

What traditional aesthetic theory is not able to understand, however, is the receptive quality of artistic experience, the manner in which the image is given to me but is shaped by my receptivity at the same time. Artists are neither geniuses nor ventriloquist's dummies; their creativity consists in entering a state of receptivity in which images can arrive and in which they can then work on these images to help them find their appropriate forms. In creative experience, artists must give up conscious control in order to be open to what is coming. They can do so not because they enter a state of mind that is exclusive to artistic genius, but precisely because they exemplify the quintessential human experience: to be open to the world.

If we maintain such a conception of artistic creativity, then there are clear implications for the use of the arts in the treatment of trauma. The art of trauma is neither a pure reproduction of the memory of an event nor a completely free rendering of it. Rather the one who is engaged in art-making, whether in a clinical or studio setting, must be open to the coming of the event in the present moment, to what images, emotions and thoughts it brings as it arrives. We could say that the art of trauma is not an imitation of the past but an opening to the future, an attempt to find a new path beyond the eternal recurrence of the same.

There is always a difference between the event and its artistic presentation. The injunction to, for example, 'Paint the trauma' is fundamentally mistaken, no matter how well intentioned. The image that comes in the art of a victim of trauma may stay close to the event or may range far from it, but it will never be entirely identified with nor divorced from the memory of what has taken place. All we can say is, 'Paint,' and if we are open, we will be surprised by what comes. The past is yet to come – that is the message which art brings and the possibility of healing that it offers. Let us hope that in our work we are worthy of receiving it.

## ON THE SENSE OF THE WORLD AS THE GROUND OF THE ARTS AND ARTS THERAPIES

I find myself in a world that makes sense. 'World' could be said to designate the totality of significance in which I dwell. This meaningful world is given to me through my senses. What comes to me in this way already has significance; I do not need to impose meaning upon it through the intellect, as modern thought would maintain.

The world in which I find myself is *our* world; it is presented to me as something that is also given to others. These others are likewise there for me, as I am for them. It is the same world that is given to us all as a meaningful whole, though within this mutuality I have a particular place, distinct from all others.

I am not, therefore, as the Cartesian world image would have it, an isolated consciousness that must somehow represent the world and others to itself; rather, I appear, as Heidegger has told us, already thrown into this world in which I live with others. It is only to the reflective ego, to the consciousness which steps back from everyday life, that the existence and meaning of the world and of others appears as a problem. The mistake of modern philosophy was to take this reflective consciousness, consciousness aware of itself and of the world as something spread out before it, as the primary datum for thought, and then to regard the existence and meaning of the world as something to be derived from my subjectivity. What is primary rather is the pre-reflective experience of life in the world, what Husserl called the *Lebenswelt* or world of everyday life. It is only on the basis of this pre-reflective experience that I can step 'outside' of the world by means of reflection.

We can also speak of the world that is created in art, that is, the imaginal reality expressed in the work. However, it would also be a mistake to take such a world as more fundamental than the life-world.

The world of the imagination that is revealed through the work of art is built upon the basis of the everyday world in which we live with others. Nevertheless the work does not 'represent' the world of everyday life. It is not an imitation (*mimesis*) of a pre-existing reality. Rather we could say that it gives a new sense to what is already meaningful, a sense in terms of which the world of everyday life now appears in a new light, one that reveals a deeper truth than our lived experience had previously given to us.

*Poiesis*, the making of a work that sets up a world, is a process of transformation; it brings something into being by shaping the world in which we live in a new way. Moreover, what is thus made could be said to 'fall back' into the world which it transforms; it becomes something which is available to us. It can therefore have an effect on us in our everyday life and can offer us the possibility of new ways of living.

How can we understand the practice of therapy, and especially the arts therapies, within this framework? Therapy is addressed to one who suffers. What then is human suffering? We could say that the one who suffers has fallen out of the world of everyday life, the meaningful totality that we share with others. In suffering, the sense of the world disappears; we can no longer take its meaning for granted, as we did before. Moreover, co-being ceases; I experience myself as alone in a meaningless world. Finally, my body, through which I am in the world in a sensible way, is experienced as alien to me. People who are ill, like the Cartesian consciousness, experience themselves as alienated from the world, from others and from their own bodies.

Therapy aims to restore the person to the ground of human existence, to the experience of embodied being in the world with others. We could therefore describe therapy as a 'rite of restoration' (Knill *et al.* 2005), as long as we understand that restoration in this context can also mean transformation. The goal of therapeutic practice is not to normalize clients but to restore to them the sense-making capacity that is intrinsic to their lives. The restoration of this 'poietic' capacity can lead to fundamental changes in the daily life of the person, changes that enable what we might call the 'singularity' of the individual to find its place in the world.

Suffering therefore can be the occasion for meaningful transformation within a therapeutic context; it can resemble the 'happy fault' (*felix culpa*) of which St. Augustine speaks, the fall that leads to deliverance. Illness, by removing me from the world, may take me deeper into myself, to a place where that which I am appears with greater force and clarity. This is why James Hillman speaks of the goal of therapy as 'soul-making' (borrowing the phrase from John Keats (2005), who remarked in a letter that the world is not a 'vale of tears' but a 'vale of Soul-making') (Hillman 1975, p.86).

What is important is not to stay within the therapeutic experience of psyche or soul. Hegel (1977) already spoke of this temptation, in his book *The Phenomenology of Spirit*, as the search for the 'beautiful soul,' for a realm of purity divorced from the tawdriness of the everyday world. For R.D. Laing (2008), this 'true self' (also described by Winnicott in 1971) can be the basis for a schizoid relationship to existence, in which only the inner self is real. In such a case, the inner self would be a fantasy designed to protect the person from the brute reality of the world.

If therapy can be seen as a realm of soul-making, it also offers the possibility of 'world-making.' The deeper truth of my existence that I find in my withdrawal from the world into the therapeutic space must be itself brought back into that very world to become effective. As Hillman himself came to see in his later work, the task of psychology is to restore soul to the world, not to create a private realm of the imagination in which I can find myself apart from the world (Hillman and Ventura 1993).

Within a therapeutic context, artistic creativity can itself be understood as a form of soul-making which aims to restore sense to the world. I take the suffering which I have undergone and look for a way to shape it, to make it present in the world in its sensible immediacy. In so doing, the truth of my suffering becomes apparent, and I can find its sense. This is the case even when this sense is only that something happened to me, something which befell me and shattered my world, as trauma does. By working with the traumatic experience I give it its shape *as* something meaningless and thereby place it within what we might call the 'fragmented totality' of my life. Otherwise the trauma remains overwhelming; it subsumes me to the extent that I become it and identify myself only as its victim. Trauma then becomes a badge of identity which defines my existence; I *am* the survivor of the trauma, not just one who has gone on living after the horrific event.

It is in being-with-others (*Mitsein*, 'being-with,' to use Heidegger's (1962) term in *Being and Time*) in the therapeutic relationship that I am able to be restored to myself and thereby transformed. The 'beautiful soul' which I discover can then appear to another; it thereby becomes a phenomenon in the world. Art-making, *poiesis*, is an especially suitable way for this to happen, since art, as we have said, is the phenomenon *par excellence*. Appearance is the essence of an art-work; it demands to be seen. The therapist is not only the one who helps make this manifestation possible, but also the one who shares in its appearance with me and thus restores to me my co-being with another in the world.

We often speak of the therapist as the witness to the work of the client, but it is important to conceive of witnessing not as detached observation but as aesthetic response. Art aims to become effective, to have an effect on others. For therapists to fulfill their role as witness, they must be open to the 'effective reality' of the work (Knill 2004), to its impact upon them, and they must be able to respond in a manner that is itself effective. This response can take the immediate form of words or gestures but it can also be fashioned aesthetically, so that there is a circle of meaning made manifest through the exchange of gifts, of what is given freely to the other. The work comes to the client as a gift, and the response by the therapist is part of the process of gift exchange that binds us to each other.

The 'sense of the world' (Nancy 1998) is the ground of the possibility of both art-making and the arts therapies. Although they may be gratifying in themselves, both these activities have a goal that transcends this gratification: to give meaning and purpose to our existence as embodied beings in the world with others. *Poiesis* is world-making. To regard it as anything less would be to take it out of its context, the nexus of meaning grounded upon the sense of the world.

## ON THE CATEGORIES OF AESTHETICS: *POIESIS, MIMESIS, CATHARSIS*

Philosophical reflection on the arts begins under the rubric of the term *poiesis*, the Greek word for making or production. For Plato, such a making is understood as a form of imitation (*mimesis*); artists imitate the thing that they see. Since within the Platonic framework, the things of this world are themselves imitations of their ideal forms or essences, the art-work is regarded by Plato as an imitation of an imitation and therefore as only a pale copy of what truly exists. Moreover, artists themselves have no knowledge of true being; they let themselves be guided by the shifting realities of the sensible world, the realm of *aisthesis* (sense-perception). Only the pure intellect can intuit the eternal and unchanging truth of being; the senses are limited to the ever-shifting flux of things that come into being and pass away.

Plato's conception seems most appropriate when he is discussing the plastic arts, in which one could see the representation of something in painting or sculpture as the goal (though that would be a limited understanding even of Greek 'representational' art). As soon as Plato turns to poetry, *mimesis* gains a different significance. Who or what do poets imitate? What is the 'thing' that they imitate? In fact, Plato's discussion of poetry, rather than demonstrating its purely imitative quality, shows that the essence of poetry is *performance*. Greek poetry, such as Homer's epics, is always performed in front of an audience; in doing so the performers enact their text, making it into a performance delivered to others. If Plato still calls this *mimesis*, then we will have to understand *mimesis* not primarily as imitation but rather as performance.

The Platonic discussion of *poiesis*, in fact, shifts according to its object. When it is a question of the visual arts, then Plato presents an argument that relies on the sense of *mimesis* as imitation. When, however, the discussion turns to poetry, *mimesis* acquires a performative dimension. This shift makes sense in terms of the different ways in which the various arts seem to present themselves and of the sensory modalities through which their reception occurs. Both painting and sculpture present themselves to our vision; they have a primarily spatial rather than temporal dimension, and at first glance they do not seem to require our active participation in order to exist. Poetry, on the other hand, as practiced in classical Greek culture, is primarily auditory; and sound can exist for us only in time, as something for which duration is intrinsic to its being. Moreover, Greek poetry must be performed in order to appear; it is not meant to be read but to be heard. Oral poetry depends for its existence upon the voice and body of the performer and also upon the presence of the audience that hears it. In Plato's text, the meaning of both *poiesis* and *mimesis* changes depending on which art form is being considered.

For Aristotle, the Platonic conception of art-making as imitation seems at first to be maintained. Tragedy is defined as the imitation (*mimesis*) of an action (*praxis*), which brings about a purification (*catharsis*) of the emotions of pity and fear. However, a reading of Aristotle's *Poetics* clearly shows that to understand the art of tragic drama, we must always keep in mind its performative character. Tragedy, even more than other forms of poetry, is enacted; in order to exist it requires that the story or plot be acted out bodily by the actors, who make it present through their words and gestures to the audience.

This sense of *poiesis* as performative recurs in Nietzsche (1967). When Nietzsche criticizes the understanding of Greek tragedy in the scholarship of his time, he points primarily to the failure to regard the texts of the tragedies as drama, as language that is meant to be presented and received in an embodied way. This failure, he feels, is what has led to the underestimation of the role of the chorus, since the song and dance that is fundamental for the chorus is absent from a reading of the texts and can only come to life in performance.

There is even a sense in which all art could be considered to be performative, as Hans-Georg Gadamer (2004 [1975]) and others have maintained. The art-work exists only in dynamic interaction with the spectator or audience. It presents itself to the audience as what it is and depends for this presentation on its actual existence. A work that is never seen exists only in potential; in fact, all works appear to someone, if only to the one who has made them, and this appearing is something that must *happen*. It is only that the performative character of the work is more easily over-looked when the work is given visually, as in a painting or literary text.

Vision is the sense that most presents its object as though it were independent of the existence of the observer. The primacy of the visual fits with a conception of being-in-the-world in terms of a subject faced with an object, something that lies before it. However, even in visual experience, the 'subject' must act for the 'object' to appear, if only by opening his or her eyes, directing the gaze and focusing on something to be seen. From a phenomenological point of view, all things that lay claim to existence are given to us through their appearances. In our experience there are no objects without subjects to whom they appear, and similarly there is no experience without something to which it is directed. In Husserl's language, every consciousness is a consciousness of something; consciousness is in that sense intentional.

Within a more fundamental conception of the person as an embodied being in the world, we could say that experience is not primarily a matter of consciousness but of sensing, *aisthesis*. The sense of the world, as I have remarked, is given to us in the first place through the senses; only on the basis of sensing is it possible to step back and engage in a reflective act of awareness. We could say therefore that our basic experience of the world is aesthetic; the world is that which is given to us through our senses. Aesthetics, then, is not only a specialized philosophical discipline but also a primary mode of existence. *We exist aesthetically.* Only because we do so is it possible to engage in *poiesis*, the performative act in which our existence manifests itself.

*Aisthesis* in its root meaning was connected with breath (Beckley and Shapiro 2002, p.271); and breath, as we know, is often identified with life. To expire is to cease to breathe, and to be inspired is to be filled with the spirit or breath. We sometimes say that an aesthetic experience is breath-taking, but it might be more accurate to say that it is breath-giving. *Poiesis* restores the body to life, it animates or ensouls it. To live in an an-aesthetic world means to be unable to breathe; it is a world without spirit or soul. And artists themselves are able to create when they are in-spired, when they are filled with the creative spirit.

Perhaps these reflections can help us gain a better understanding of *catharsis*, the purifying act which *poiesis* brings about. Aristotle says that tragedy brings *catharsis*, a word that signifies 'purification.' The term 'purification' can have a medical meaning; in that sense, catharsis implies the elimination of a toxic substance from the body, for example through purging. However, the term also can have a religious significance; to purify a person, place or object is to make it holy. What is purified in this sense is not expelled but transformed; its profane qualities are rendered sacred. The effect of tragic drama for Aristotle is not to expel pity and fear or terror but to transform them into compassion and awe. We do not leave the theater purged of what makes us weak; on the contrary, the experience of tragedy makes us realize our fellow-feeling with the one who suffers and leaves us with a sense of the magnificence of the power that rules our lives.

Classical Greek culture is founded on the myth of the hero, the one who by cunning and force overcomes insurmountable obstacles. Tragedy, to the contrary, shows us the failure or lack to which the hero's striving has led him; it is his very virtue or power that has brought about his downfall. Oedipus is the classic example, the hero who has saved Thebes through the power of his intellect and rules it through his will. These are the qualities which, when pursued to their logical conclusion, result in his ruin. In the end, he leaves the city as one who is both blind and helpless. It is only at the end of his life that his final resting-place can become sacred to the gods and a benefit to humans.

When we exit the theater, we are restored to life. The breath-taking drama gives us back our capacity to breathe. We have undergone a ritual act in which our ego or 'I,' the subject of knowledge and will, is laid low, but in which for that very reason our lives are re-animated. By accepting the fate of Oedipus through its aesthetic presentation in the tragic drama, we are brought back to the ground of our existence in our ongoing life. No more than Oedipus can we overcome our mortal lives, our finitude and our dependence upon powers greater than ourselves. We return to the body, the breath, and the others with whom we dwell on this earth. This is the effect of *poiesis*, the *mimesis* that works through *aisthesis* to bring about *catharsis*, the purification and sanctification of human life.

## ON TRAUMA AND TRAGEDY

Trauma is defined by repetition; the original event recurs as flashback or intrusive memory. In that sense we could say that trauma is akin to tragedy, defined as the imitation of an action that has already taken place. This does not mean that the traumatic repetition, any more than the dramatic one, is a blind or mechanical reproduction of its prototype. Repetition introduces difference; we play something again but never in the same way twice. Whether by intention or not, the traumatic as well as the tragic repetition brings something new into our experience, all the more so since we ourselves are no longer the same. A traumatic experience relived years later comes to a person who is in a different position in life, within a different context, and who experiences what has happened to him differently according to his new place in the world.

What happens then, to the art of trauma if it is not a pure representation of an event? If the art of trauma is tragedy, then tragic art could be considered trauma-play; it is a way of 'playing' at something that makes it more real for us. The purpose of this play is not to restore a pre-existing harmony, nor to master the event and therefore overcome it, but rather to remember it by imagining it more deeply.

In the arts, we remember by imagining, and this is possible because memory itself is the shaping of the experience of an event, with all the selection, emphasis and amplification that shaping implies. 'I remember' really means, 'I re-create'; I play it again in a different way. Moreover, if artistic representation is not mere repetition, this is because there is, as we have noted, already a shaping element in my lived experience. Even for the child, there is not a passive imprinting on her consciousness by an 'external' world. The child engages in an active responding to the impingements of the environment (a process common to all organisms) that gradually gives rise to a certain 'style' of response that becomes typical of that particular person. This active response is carried out at a pre-reflective level of experience and does not imply conscious choice, though it may serve later as something to consciously assent to or struggle against (as when a fearful person tries to overcome his anxieties).

The ego or conscious 'I' may defend itself against traumatic experience, through denial, projection or some other defense mechanism, as we know. At the most basic level, we could even see the ego itself as a defense: the creation of a split in the subject so that a reflective distance from the wound is possible. The experience of art, on the other hand, requires a breaching of the defenses of the ego and, in the most powerful cases, even a dismantling of the ego itself. In a powerful artistic experience, we are overwhelmed and have to surrender. In some ways this mimics the effect of the trauma that overwhelmed us in the past; however, in this case the dissolution of the ego produces joy and not terror. Thus tragic art is an experience akin to orgasm in that we must surrender our separateness and yield to something greater than ourselves. We return then to the body-self that predates our egoic existence, the pure flow of life itself. Only such an account of our experience can do justice to the phenomenon of 'tragic joy,' the way in which the artistic representation of the most painful suffering can bring the greatest pleasure. This tragic joy in the dissolution of the individual is what Nietzsche calls the 'Dionysian,' his name for the process of creation and destruction that constitutes the essence of life.

We might say that traumatic suffering and ecstatic joy are the 'same' in that they both involve an annihilation of the ego. The difference is that tragedy is *play*, and in this play there is the emergence of meaning where previously there had only been brute fact. In the performative *mimesis*, the symbolic dimension emerges without being a pure product of interpretation by a reflective consciousness. The emerging symbolic meaning transcends explanation into categories; it strikes us immediately and is charged with affect. The symbol is half-way between the concept and the fact; it has particular existence yet is also significant. We can reflect upon it afterwards – as Paul Ricoeur (1969, p.347) has said, 'The symbol gives rise to thought' – but in itself the symbol strikes us in a pre-reflective way at the level of our lived existence. It requires more than the act of an ego in order to exist.

To account for the effect of either trauma or tragedy, we need a conception of human nature that is not based on the primacy of the ego or of consciousness. Merleau-Ponty (1964) speaks of 'the primacy of perception,' but perhaps we could say it is a matter of the primacy of 'existence' or 'life.' The arts plunge us back into an experience of living which is meaningful in itself, though this meaning is given to us in ways that cannot be clearly articulated. Kant (1996), in his theory of knowledge, said that perceptions without concepts are blind, but this position makes sense only if we uncritically accept the Cartesian oppositions between body and mind and between subject and object, oppositions which are founded in a reflective apprehension of the self as a self-conscious being, a 'thinking thing,' in Descartes's terms. If we begin instead with a conception of the self as an embodied being that encounters the world through its senses, then we can see perception as already sensible, that is, filled with sense or meaning.

Tragedy works because it produces *catharsis*, a pre-reflective experience of the purification of the soul. The soul is animated through tragic play; it returns to the life that had been extinguished in it through its suffering. Yet now it is a life that can encompass that suffering; it is, we might say, an 'active passivity,' choosing to undergo in play an experience which rids the ego of its agency and therefore renders it helpless.

In the tragic drama, the hero wins by losing; Oedipus becomes blessed only when everything has been taken away from him. The spectator shares this experience of loss by giving up the reflective distance with which she ordinarily regards the world. The 'spectator' becomes a 'participant.' Although the tragic performances, performed at Dionysian festivals, were sometimes said by the Greeks themselves to have 'nothing to do with Dionysos' (Winkler and Zeitlin 1990), there is a sense in which they are similar to religious rituals, in which what is sacrificed becomes holy. We must 'surrender' to the play, as Oedipus surrendered to his fate; only then can we too become blessed.

Ultimately tragedy requires that we surrender to death, to the inevitability of mortal existence. When Conrad (2001, p.137) wrote, 'The horror! The horror!', he expressed the awe-filled character of life, the realization that death is not extrinsic to life but at its core. Rilke later said that he saw his task as a poet to be to 'love life so generously...that we involuntarily come to include, and to love, death too' (Mitchell 1989, p.331). We might say that this is the task of tragedy and, perhaps, of all art.

The ego exists as a principle of immortality; it considers itself to be infinite, without boundaries, and therefore strives for omniscience and omnipotence. Entire civilizations have been built on that premise, and, indeed, perhaps civilization itself requires such a belief in order to function. Trauma shatters this illusion of knowledge and control; the ego is defeated in trauma, it can neither comprehend nor master what has happened. A natural way of responding to trauma then would be to attempt to restore the *status quo ante*, the stable persona that masks the chaotic flux of life. However, such a response would mean that we have remained ignorant, that we have learned nothing from the experience and therefore will be likely to repeat it, either to ourselves or to others. We run the risk of repeating the trauma rather than going beyond it.

Tragic wisdom, on the contrary, encompasses the finitude of existence. It is an affirmation of existence that sees suffering and death as intrinsic to it and nevertheless says 'Yes!' to life. Such wisdom is not rational knowledge, not anything we can analyze and justify by logical reasoning. Rather, it is the result of a transformative experience that, we can say, sanctifies us without the necessity of a divine being to intervene in our lives. The way to redeem trauma is as tragedy; only in this way can we avoid repeating it. Instead we can remember and even, perhaps, accept.

# 3

# Mimetic Wounds

## *From Trauma to Tragedy*

Psychotherapy has been traumatized: it shows all the symptoms of the trauma victim, suffering from thoughts that are intrusive and constrictive and that tend to hyper-vigilance. What has produced this condition, oddly enough, is the discourse of trauma itself. This discourse intrudes upon our theory and practice even when we wish to think or act otherwise; it constricts us by rendering other forms of suffering opaque. We are always on the alert for trauma, seeing it behind every symptom, as if they were all traumas in disguise.

In *Trauma: A Genealogy* (2000), Ruth Leys has written what she calls a 'genealogy' of the discourse of trauma, not a continuous narrative but an analysis of certain key episodes in the history of trauma theory which reveal its inner structure – a structure marked, in her view, by an irresolvable contradiction. Her book is the most sophisticated and comprehensive account of the theory of trauma that has been written. We need to look closely at it in order to move toward a better formulation of a theory of trauma.

For Leys, the central contradiction of all trauma theories 'may be seen to revolve around *the problem of imitation, defined as a problem of hypnotic identification*' (Leys 2000, p.8, emphasis hers). From the beginning, the discourse of trauma was associated with imitation (*mimesis*) and hypnosis. As Leys notes:

> This is because the tendency of hypnotized persons to imitate or repeat whatever they were told to say or do provided a basic model for the traumatic experience. Trauma was defined as a situation of dissociation or 'absence' from the self in which the victim unconsciously imitated, or identified with, the aggressor

or traumatic scene in a condition that was likened to a state
of heightened suggestibility or hypnotic trance. Trauma was
therefore understood as an experience of hypnotic imitation
or identification – what I call *mimesis* – an experience that,
because it appeared to shatter the victim's cognitive-perceptual
capacities, made the traumatic scene unavailable for a certain
kind of recollection. (Leys 2000, p.8)

What makes trauma a mimetic problem is that trauma victims tend
to 'repeat' the original wound, whether in the form of nightmares,
flashbacks, obsessive thoughts and images or other symptoms. Unlike
others who have suffered from psychic wounds, the victim of trauma
seems unable to 'represent' the trauma through an act of memory. The
mimetic identification with the trauma was thus understood, in theories
of trauma, as preventing the necessary distance for a cognitive awareness
of what had happened. As in post-hypnotic suggestion, the trauma victim
was viewed as having no conscious recollection of her experience; this
was because, as in hypnosis, she was not consciously present while
the event was happening. The overwhelming character of the traumatic
event was understood to exceed the ability of the traumatized person
to grasp it cognitively. Instead, she could only identify with the event
without being able to distance herself from it.

However, as Leys (2000, p.9) shows, 'a tendency towards the
repudiation of *mimesis* was from the start also at work in the field.' The
mimetic theory, after all, threatened the 'ideal of individual autonomy
and responsibility' that is necessary for the integrity of the person.
Trauma victims risked being conceived as less than moral subjects
when seen through the lens of *mimesis*. Furthermore, if the trauma is
a mimetic phenomenon, is not the victim somehow complicit in the
event, even if only by surrendering her autonomy? And if trauma is like
hypnotic suggestion, then is it not also possible that the trauma victim
will be suspected of fabricating her wound, suggestively inducing the
symptoms from which she suffers?

For these and other reasons, the mimetic theory immediately gave
rise to an anti-mimetic position, according to which the trauma is
understood as a purely external event that comes to the victim from the
'outside' and for which, therefore, she is in no way responsible. This
anti-mimetic position implies that the victim was, unlike the hypnotic
subject, present during the traumatic event, although the shock was so
overwhelming that all memory of it was erased from awareness. This

means that the event can, in principle, become available for conscious recollection, not only for mimetic repetition. The contrasting theories of trauma thus led to different kinds of therapeutic action. On the one hand, a mimetic conception of trauma implies that the effects of the trauma can only be overcome by an abreactive enactment or purging (*catharsis*) of emotion; on the other hand, the anti-mimetic theory leads to the notion that the goal of therapy is the recovery of memory in order to produce a narrative representation, a conscious integration of the traumatic experience into the continuity of a life history.

This opposition between conflicting theoretical paradigms would not be troubling were it not the fact that, as Leys shows, the opposition occurs not only between rival theories but within each of the opposing theoretical positions as well. There is thus a 'tension or oscillation between the two paradigms'; each calls forth the other so that neither can stand alone (Leys 2000, p.10). Leys demonstrates, by a close reading of the texts of the relevant thinkers (from Freud and Morton Prince to Bessel A. van der Kolk and Cathy Caruth), that every attempt to resolve or overcome the opposition between *mimesis* and anti-mimesis ends in failure. For her this demonstrates a structural contradiction in the discourse of trauma itself. Her genealogy thus becomes a deconstructive or critical account of the history of trauma theory: it aims at revealing the contradictions in a discourse that lays claim to authoritative knowledge.

In this respect, Leys stands in the tradition of Michel Foucault, for whom a genealogical account was never neutral. Its goal was always to reveal the ways in which the structure of knowledge constitutive of a particular epoch contained the operation of a particular kind of power. For example, the concept of madness constitutive of the Age of Enlightenment (and, to some extent, of our own epoch as well) could not in Foucault's view be understood without inserting it into a structural opposition to sanity, which resulted in the exclusion of the insane from normal society by means of the invention of the asylum, conceived of as a humane form of treatment for the mentally ill. The form of knowledge that is necessary for the construction of a 'rational' society thus depends on the exclusion and banishment of those who are regarded as irrational or insane (and of others deemed abnormal as well, e.g. the ill, criminals, the poor, the elderly, and so on). This produces a situation radically different from pre-modern societies, in which the mad were considered to have a necessary place in the social order.

What then does Leys see as the 'power' of traumatic knowledge? How does the discourse of trauma construct the subject of traumatic experience so that her position is inscribed differently in the social and political world? For Leys, the answer is clear: trauma theory, structured by the opposition between *mimesis* and anti-mimesis, produces a traumatized subject, one who is absolved of all responsibility for her acts. The traumatized person is re-conceived as a helpless victim, one to whom inconceivably bad things have happened. Hence traumatic experience, rather than inducing shame (often the experience of victims of trauma) can lead to the valorization of the condition of the victim. To be a victim is, henceforth, a badge of honor. We have all been, as Cathy Caruth (1995) would indicate, the victims of a history that we did not make. The concept of trauma tends to spread by a contagious process so that even those who were not directly involved in the traumatic event are nevertheless infected. 'Trauma' then becomes the way in which identity in general is configured: we are all victims.

For Leys, this 'traumatization' of history runs the risk of eliminating moral responsibility. Even the perpetrator must be re-conceived as a victim who acts out his victimization through acts of violence (thus the common conception that the abuser must have himself been a victim of abuse). This is, as Ian Hacking (1996, p.71) has pointed out, a kind of 'memoro-politics,' in which we are conceived as being constituted by what we have forgotten (in this case, the traumatic wound). Leys' genealogical account (in spite of her wish to view herself as one who does not take sides) is clearly a critique of this memory politics and is, thus, in my opinion, itself a political act.

This comes out most clearly in her attack on the 'literalist' account of trauma implicit in those theories that try to establish themselves on an anti-mimetic basis. For the neurobiologist Bessel A. van der Kolk (1996), as well as, interestingly, for the deconstructive literary critic, Cathy Caruth (1996), who builds on his theories, the traumatic memory is a literal reproduction of the event, stored in a different memory system than that of normal 'narrative' or 'declarative' memory (cf. Antze and Lambek 1996). Leys shows the shaky evidence for this position, as well as the contradictions implicit in it; but it is clear, as she herself admits, that her critical analysis here has an edge that is absent from her other chapters. Leys obviously does not want to be caught in the logic of victimization to which the 'literalist' basis of the anti-mimetic account leads.

In this respect, her analysis echoes that of Nietzsche, the progenitor of the genealogical method. In *On The Genealogy of Morals*, Nietzsche (1996) tried to show that the opposition between 'good' and 'evil' which structures the moral discourse of the Christian world is based on an inversion of the earlier distinction between 'good' and 'bad', characteristic of the heroic period of Greek culture. In the classical Greek moral universe, the values of the 'good,' those who are the masters of society, are distinguished from the characteristics of the 'bad,' those who occupy an inferior position. The dominant values of strength, vitality, physical courage and sensual pleasure are associated with the superior position of those who rule and are thereby given first place in the scale of values. Those who are inferior emulate these virtues and covet their position.

With the advent of Christianity, in Nietzsche's view, there is a 'transvaluation of values,' in which the characteristics of inferior groups become prized as the very hallmark of morality: humility, poverty, chastity, obedience, self-denial (all despised by the 'masters' as badges of inferiority) become the qualities of the 'good.' Henceforth, the values associated with the powerful are seen as characteristic of evil (pride, ambition, aggression, sexuality, and so on.) Christianity for Nietzsche is thus a 'slave religion'; it espouses the virtues of the powerless out of a spirit of *ressentiment* toward the masters of the world.

Foucault, then, is Nietzsche's heir; his genealogy of knowledge is designed to show the conceptual framework that structures the subject of power, a framework that, in fact, disciplines her so that she willingly embraces the loss of her own freedom (Foucault 2002). Does not Leys' analysis follow in this tradition? To be a victim today is to have the only secure moral status possible. The subject constructed as the victim of trauma is valorized by her helplessness and powerlessness. It will not escape the reader that the victim of trauma is conceived by trauma theory in terms that have traditionally been used to represent the feminine. Leys' genealogical critique could, then, be read as a feminist refusal to espouse a misogynist conception of women.

What, then, of *mimesis*? It is clear that Leys is partial to mimetic accounts, even when she shows the problems that arise from them. In part, she bases her analysis on the work of Mikkel Borch-Jacobsen, whose early writings on Freud revealed a mimetic concept of identity underlying his conception of the Oedipal subject (Borch-Jacobsen 1993). In Freud's framework, for Borch-Jacobsen, before libidinal attachment (which requires a subject capable of desiring an object), there is an 'emotional tie' which binds the self immediately to another. This primary identification or *mimesis* is repeated in group psychology, as well as in the transference. It is, essentially, a hypnotic tie, like the one that links the hypnotized person to the hypnotist. Hypnosis, transference and group psychology, along with other phenomena, are themselves all conceivable as states of trance. For Borch-Jacobsen, psychoanalysis, which began by banishing hypnosis from its therapeutic arsenal, is in fact based on a theory and practice centered on the experience of trance.

In *The Emotional Tie: Psychoanalysis, Mimesis, and Affect*, Borch-Jacobsen (1993) gives an analysis of trance based on the anthropological writings of Luc de Heusch on spirit possession in 'primitive' societies. De Heusch shows that in these societies, illness is conceived of as a form of aggression, caused by a sorcerer or spirit. Thus, in Borch-Jacobsen's presentation of the theory:

> Illness consists in a possession of the soul by a malefic spirit or substance, a possession that consequently calls for an *abreactive* or *exorcist* procedure, since the malefic influence must be expelled, or in a *dispossession* of the soul, which thus requires a procedure that de Heusch calls *adreactive* or *adorcist*, by means of which the soul is returned to its rightful owner. (Borch-Jacobsen 1993, p.103, italics in original)

Both possession and dispossession are ways, says Borch-Jacobsen (1993, p.104), of conceiving the 'brutal collapse of the boundaries between "self" and "other."' In other words, they result from a process of mimetic identification. What is most interesting, for our purposes, is that in 'primitive' societies, the cure for possession is itself mimetic – it works by inducing a state of trance in which the experience of *mimesis* is dramatized. This dramatization, in which either the sufferer or the healer becomes the possessing spirit and dramatically enacts the story, results in the healing of the illness and, often, a conversion of the malevolent demon into a beneficent power. Sometimes, in fact, the sufferer is able to utilize the power of the spirit to become a healer himself. Thus *mimesis*, which first produced an abject identification with the possessing spirit, becomes, as dramatic identification, the means of cure.

Borch-Jacobsen relates the role of *mimesis* in these cultures to its place in psychoanalysis. In *The Emotional Tie* and other early writings, Borch-Jacobsen gives a favorable portrayal of the Freudian subject from

the point of view of *mimesis*, both in terms of the formation of this subject
in the earliest emotional tie and in the identificatory *mimesis* which is,
in spite of Freud's attempt to banish it, at the heart of the transference
phenomenon as well as in its cure. Leys' analysis of Freud tends to echo
this valorization. She is, therefore, somewhat understandably dismayed
by Borch-Jacobsen's later writings, in which he abandons psychoanalysis
and revises the concept of *mimesis* itself (Borch-Jacobsen 1997).

However, this turn in Borch-Jacobsen's thinking actually contains
a clue that may help us to think about *mimesis* differently. In his earlier
work, Borch-Jacobsen based his conception of *mimesis* on the model
of hypnosis espoused by Freud and his contemporaries, according to
which the subject is absent from the hypnotic trance, which occurs
without his conscious awareness. The subject of hypnosis (and therefore
of all 'hypnoid' states) could therefore be said to be 'blind.' The goal of
analysis would then be to enable this subject to see — that is, to acquire
'insight' into her condition.

Subsequently, and partly through his own experience of Eriksonian
hypnosis, Borch-Jacobsen revised his earlier theory and came to
the conclusion that hypnosis, as well as any other state of trance, is
accompanied by a conscious awareness and willingness on the part of
the subject. Hypnosis thus can be conceived of as a *game*, willingly
entered into by both parties, in which the subject agrees to *simulate*
her experience in accordance with the rules of the game, as contracted
with the hypnotist. Borch-Jacobsen (1997) was therefore led to reject
psychoanalysis as a kind of fraud.

What is significant for us is not so much the critique of psychoanalysis
(which seems rather simplistic) as the introduction of a nuance into the
concept of *mimesis*. To conceive of *mimesis* as 'simulation,' rather than
reducing mimetic phenomena to the realm of fraudulent behavior,
seems to me to restore the concept to its rightful role. *Mimesis* is, in
fact, a *dramatic* phenomenon, as Borch-Jacobsen himself acknowledges;
as we have noted, the concept itself arises in the analysis of dramatic
presentation in Plato, particularly in *The Republic*. It then repeats itself in
the *Poetics* of Aristotle, where it is used to define the essence of tragedy.
From the perspective of a theory of dramatic imitation, however,
*mimesis* appears differently than in a theory based on the concept of
identification.

If we recognize the *dramatic* origin of *mimesis*, then perhaps our
understanding of the mimetic character of trauma can itself be re-

configured. In drama, *mimesis* is both conscious and enacted; there is thus none of the opposition between 'blind' enactment and 'conscious' recollection that structures the discourse of trauma. In fact, one might say that trauma is a form of failed *mimesis*. In trauma, imitation is reduced to identification, and the distance that is necessary to recognize the mimetic performance is abolished.

The distinction between imitation and identification is important, for it leads to a new alternative for therapeutic practice. Rather than having to choose between abreaction and recollection, between a blind enactment which 'repeats' an act of identification and a conscious representation which claims to 'integrate' the traumatic event into the narrative of one's life (an impossible alternative, as Leys shows), there emerges the possibility of *conscious enactment*, in other words, the dramatic re-presentation of the traumatic event, its shaping in artistic form. Artistic or poetic *mimesis* is always a kind of shaping. *Mimesis* is in fact an interpretive practice; its 'repetition' is always a 're-presentation.' This is clear in the experience of theater; it is absurd to think that theatrical performance is a literal reproduction of anything whatsoever. Moreover, each production 'differs' from every other even in the performance of the 'same' work; indeed, successive performances of the same production will always differ as well.

*Mimesis is not identification.* The same is not the identical. *Mimesis* cannot be thought within the logic of identification in which one is either oneself or another. If there is a concept that can capture the essence of the mimetic process, it is that of *resemblance* rather than identification. This means that a mimetic or imitative act is neither identical with nor different from its 'object' (and, of course, outside of a logic of identity, there can be neither subject nor object, at least not in the traditional sense of these terms). Rather a mimetic act is *like* what it imitates. The mimetic performance resembles its object, but it is not identical with it. In this respect it obeys the logic of resemblance rather than that of identity.

This is, in fact, one of the bases of Plato's rejection of *mimesis*. The poets must be banished from the just city, since their *poiesis* is based on *seeming* rather than on *being*. That is, the mimetic basis of *poiesis* renders it antagonistic to philosophy, which requires knowledge of what is, not imitation of what only appears to be. The fact that Plato was unable to banish *mimesis* from his own thinking is evidence enough that this distinction, on which the very project of philosophy is based, is itself suspect. The advent of phenomenology was merely the last step in the philosophical restoration of the realm of appearance or seeming – a restoration already present in every work of art.

The discourse of trauma is traumatizing because it repeats the traumatic structure: the split between being and knowing in which no mediation is possible. Leys herself unwittingly repeats (as trauma invariably does) the terms of this discourse by her 'close reading' of the relevant texts. As Borch-Jacobsen was later to say about his own early analysis of Freud,

> this is what the strategy of deconstruction is all about: you take a theory and use its own conceptuality to highlight its internal contradictions, aporias, etc. But when you engage in this kind of parasitic activity, you obviously run the risk of becoming yourself a victim of the conceptuality you feed upon. (Borch-Jacobsen 1997, p.216)

Though genealogy is not the same as deconstruction, this description applies to Leys' analysis as well. Despite her critique of memoro-politics, she repeats the theoretical aporia contained in the traumatic conception of *mimesis*. Her discourse is in fact constituted by an opposition between a close reading, in which she identifies with her texts, and a critical analysis, in which she maintains the specular distance necessary for the practitioner of genealogy.

To go 'beyond' the structural opposition of *mimesis* and anti-mimesis, it is necessary to restore the original place of *mimesis* as the essence of *poiesis*. Not only will this help us to envision trauma differently (perhaps even the concept of 'trauma' will have to be incorporated within a broader category of social suffering), but also therapeutic practice itself will have other alternatives than the mere 'pragmatism' of techniques, which Leys' demonstration of the inadequacy of trauma theory leads her to recommend at the end of her book.

*Mimesis/poiesis/catharsis* – the ancient terms need to be 'repeated' and therefore understood differently in order to become the basis of contemporary therapeutic practice. One way for this to happen is to re-vision the healing practices of traditional cultures from the point of view of an understanding of dramatic performance as enacted in Greek tragic theatre. There is a relationship (of resemblance, not of identity) between traditional performances of healing and dramatic enactment on the tragic stage that enables the concept of *catharsis* to be used in both a therapeutic and a theatrical sense. The *mimesis* of *poiesis* produces *catharsis* – the classical formula holds true, provided we do not interpret it within the antinomies of classical thought.

The key to a therapeutic practice based on the arts lies in a re-thinking of the concept of *mimesis* that is at the heart of *poiesis*. How can we understand *mimesis* without reducing it to a form of identification? Perhaps if we think it from the point of view of *poiesis* itself, it will appear differently than when it is conceived in terms of a philosophical analysis based on the logic of conceptual thought. *Poiesis* has a *logos* of its own. The poietic is not without thought, but its thinking is embodied. The corporeal logic of *poiesis* requires the bodily presence of performance in order to be realized. *Poiesis* is performative. That is why we must speak of the performance of healing; for *poiesis* to occur, it must be enacted.

The difficulty, it seems to me, is that we continue to conceive of *mimesis* in terms of identification. As long as we operate within the logic of identity (in which thought and being, mind and body, self and other, stand in opposition), we will always fall back into the antinomies of blind identification and specular representation, immediacy and distance. The whole project of contemporary thought is to overcome these antinomies by developing a mode of thinking differently, a way of thinking the middle realm 'between' the oppositions of traditional logic. The work of such thinkers as Merleau-Ponty, Deleuze, Derrida, Serres, Lacoue-Labarthe and Nancy can all be thought of as performances that resemble each other in the staging of a post-modern world, a world which 'repeats' (differently) the pre-philosophical worlds of traditional cultures in which *poiesis* is recognized as a form of knowing, a tragic wisdom that leads to responsibility by the acceptance of suffering.

To say this is not to recommend primitivism, nor to attempt to return to the early Greeks. Such an identificatory *mimesis* could only end in unwitting self-parody. Rather, we need to look at post-modern performance and the performance of post-modernity to see how *poiesis* 'repeats' itself today. In this sense, the deconstructive critique of a 'metaphysics of presence' (the attempt to find an unchanging ground for thought) (Derrida 1997, p.309) needs to be continually repeated if we are to develop a poietic phenomenology, free of all fundamentalisms, that could lead to a theory, a way of seeing, capable of responding to the trauma of our times.

To be neither victim nor executioner, we need to move into the middle realm in which we can play out our lives differently. Trauma is not only a mimetic wound; it is the wounding of *mimesis* itself. The identificatory incorporation of suffering can be overcome only by its mimetic embodiment in a performative or playful mode. Drama and trauma are thus indissolubly linked. Indeed, trauma could itself be considered drama, but in the form of a blind enactment of suffering (this is why we can speak of a 'tragic' event). To overcome trauma is not to be achieved through the establishment of a specular differentiation that provides a vantage point from which it can be surveyed and mastered. Rather the *catharsis* of healing comes only through a poetic *mimesis* in which I can enact my suffering without becoming it.

If psychotherapy has indeed been wounded by the discourse of trauma, then we need to re-play this discourse differently. Otherwise therapy itself will become the trauma from which we seek to escape. It remains to be seen whether therapeutic discourse can regain a poietic dimension or whether it will become hostile to the arts. In that case, we can only hope that the spirit of *poiesis* will find another stage on which to perform its healing acts.

4

# Trauma, Therapy and the Arts

## *Towards a Dionysian* Poiesis

### THE TRAUMA OF PSYCHOTHERAPY

History repeats itself. For victims of trauma, the repetition seems endless. They experience themselves as re-living the traumatic experience again and again. The repetition comes against their will, insisting its way into awareness and dominating the field of consciousness, thereby inhibiting other possibilities of thought and action. Trauma never gives up. How can it be overcome?

In recent years, trauma has come to dominate the consciousness not only of the victim (of rape, abuse, war, etc.) but also of the whole field of psychotherapy. Therapy has been redefined as the healing of traumatic wounds. Human suffering is thereby understood under the sign of trauma; healing means the overcoming of traumatic memories. In a sense, we could say that psychotherapy itself has come to resemble the victim of trauma: it is obsessed with painful past events, haunted by traumatic memories and hyper-vigilant about their occurrence, and limited in its capacity to imagine alternatives. There is a mimetic quality in the therapeutic conception of trauma that is like the experience of the trauma survivor.

In a way, all discourse on the subject of *mimesis* runs the risk of becoming mimetic. *Mimesis* itself is contagious. Indeed, mimetic phenomena are often conceived as forms of contagion, for example, hysteria, mob panic. They can also be seen as a kind of hypnosis, an unconscious identification with the will of the other. It is no accident that Freud 'discovered' hysteria through his involvement in hypnosis. If trauma tends to traumatize – and trauma workers are constantly warned about 'secondary' traumatization – then this tendency stems from its mimetic origin.

There is something happening here that has an uncanny character. Indeed the uncanny itself can be seen as having a mimetic quality – something returns, a *revenant*, a ghost. It haunts us without our understanding; we become terrified, immobilized by it. This double, *Doppelgänger*, shadow, recurs without our willing it. History repeats itself – *déjà vu* all over again.

What, then, is *mimesis* that it returns again, returns in experience and returns in discourse? How can we think it without repeating it? How, in other words, can we escape from the shadow of the past, the nightmare of history (as Joyce said) from which we are trying to awake? In this chapter, we will attempt to think *mimesis* differently, to see whether even in the repetition which *mimesis* brings, difference is possible. We need to look more closely at memory. Is memory a reproduction of the past or does it necessarily include within it something that leads into the future? Can imagination remain faithful to memory and still find its wings? What role could the arts play in coming to terms with history? Is there a specific form of *poiesis* that is appropriate to a coming to terms with the past? How can we understand the *mimesis* of trauma without remaining trapped in a traumatic conception?

## TRAUMA, *MIMESIS* AND MEMORY

To say that trauma is figured mimetically in therapeutic discourse is to say that the experience of suffering is understood thereby as having an inherently mimetic quality. Trauma repeats itself; it recurs against our will; it presents itself as always the same – the same violation, the same pain and humiliation. It cannot be expelled; it is like a foreign body that has taken up residence in the self. War memories, memories of rape and abuse, all come back as 'flashbacks,' as if they were happening again. The past is literally repeated. At least this is the current understanding of trauma in trauma discourse. The *mimesis* of trauma is understood to be absolute repetition, a recurrence of the same. The traumatic act is seen as leaving an indelible trace in the mind (later, the 'brain'). *Mimesis* re-plays itself without difference.

This understanding of the quality of *mimesis* as blind repetition in trauma theory is itself founded in (or is a mimetic repetition of) the experience of the victim. The trauma victim indeed feels as if the unwanted memory is an exact duplication of the past event; the victim feels haunted by the ghost of the past. To question the validity of the memory therefore becomes tantamount to an invalidation of the victim's experience, thereby perpetuating the cycle of abuse.

However, this conception of the *mimesis* involved in trauma is problematic. Absolutely compelling traumatic memories have often been disputed, not only by reference to what 'really' happened, but also by other equally compelling competing memories of the event. Moreover, this difficulty is obvious in the case of memory in general, as the famous unreliability of the eye-witness in criminal trials has demonstrated again and again. Trauma theories have had to argue for a special character belonging to traumatic memories as distinct from other memories, in order to substantiate their own conception of the mimetic reality of the traumatic experience. I think the difficulty here stems in part from an inability to distinguish the experience of trauma victims from the truth of their testimony. Unless this distinction is made, the conclusion follows that the memories must be literally true. To contest this conclusion would then imply that the experience of trauma did not actually occur, an unacceptable alternative (as when 'shell-shocked' war veterans were accused of malingering).

One way out of this dilemma is to take a phenomenological attitude, in which the existence of the phenomenon is held in suspension and attention is paid instead to the way that it is given in awareness. It does seem that trauma victims experience their memories as absolutely veridical; the memories come with the quality of 'having happened exactly like this.' That is why it is so painful for the validity of these memories to be put into question. To do so seems like an attempt to deny the memory itself, and this feels like a callous disregard for, even denial of, the suffering to which the memory refers.

It would make sense, in fact, to see memory as a literal repetition of the past, if the past were once a present in which something was mimetically represented. In other words, memory can be conceived mimetically only when perception is understood in the same way. If our present experience is a 'copy' or 'model' of the world, then of course its recall would be a copy as well – the copy of a copy, to speak in Platonic terms. But clearly the copy theory of perception is suspect, not only from a critique of its epistemological status or from its partaking in the 'metaphysics of presence' that has dominated Western thought, but primarily because perception is not given to us in experience in this manner. The perceptual experience does not present itself as a copy of anything whatsoever, but as a direct presentation of the world. The world is given as presented to us in perception, not re-presented as in memory.

Moreover, in the perceptual presentation of the world, the involvement of the perceiver in the act of perception is also given. As we have pointed out, in order to see, I must open my eyes. In addition, I must turn my attention in a certain direction; if I look elsewhere, I will see something different. Moreover, I must focus on the object of sight; even within a given field of vision, I can concentrate on one or another figure, reducing the alternatives to background. This involvement is even more evident with respect to senses other than sight. I must move my body in order to touch something, or admit an object to my mouth to taste it. Even perceptions that come without my volition are partially subject to my behavior – I can 'close my nose' to avoid the noxious smell or, failing that, at least remove myself from the area in which the smell will affect me.

Experiments in Gestalt psychology only confirm the phenomenological evidence: perceptual experience includes an active, shaping component as well as a passive, receptive one. Of course, I cannot create a perceptual object by my intention alone; it is presented as given to me, not created by me (in contrast to the way in which the imaginal object appears). But unless I co-operate in the experience, the perceptual object will also not become manifest.

The same quality of involvement adheres to memory. In the first place, from a phenomenological perspective, what I remember is never the event itself; it is the event as experienced by me. Moreover, even the event as experienced is not remembered in the form of an identical copy. I only remember moments of my experience of an event – otherwise my memory would take as long as the event itself, which would be absurd. I remember what stands out for me; I can 'search my memory'; I can re-call experiences I am not currently thinking of. Memory needs the one who remembers, even if that one is not a reflectively aware, self-conscious ego. Ordinary memory, in other words, requires intentionality.

Let us look more closely at the traumatic concept of memory. There is no such thing as 'trauma,' if trauma is taken as an 'in-itself.' One could even make the categorical statement that no event is in itself inherently traumatic; it must be experienced as traumatic to become a trauma. This may seem self-evident, but in fact it is a highly contested statement. It implies not only that a 'small' event may be experienced in a traumatic way ('the cold manner in which you said goodbye that day') but also that something very 'large' might not be traumatic at all. Otherwise, the fact that not all combat veterans suffer from post-traumatic stress disorder would be inexplicable. Even rape or sexual abuse is not necessarily experienced as traumatic, if by 'trauma' we mean an event which results in memories that repeat themselves endlessly, compulsively and intrusively. By no means am I implying that these events do not cause suffering, even unbearable suffering; but that is a different matter from defining them as 'traumatic,' in the sense of the term under discussion.

Therefore we must be aware that when we say 'trauma,' we are really saying, 'the experience of trauma' or 'the event as experienced traumatically.' This enables us to get beyond the question of belief when trying to understand traumatic experience. (Of course, we will never get beyond this question when we must determine what actually happened, as in courts of law or war-crimes tribunals.)

Traumatic experience happens *as if* it were an identical repetition of the original event. It is not necessary to convert this subjunctive tense into the indicative in order to honor the experience of the victim. By adapting a literal notion of mimetic identification, trauma theory seems to me to have become infected by the contagious mimetic quality of the experience it focuses on. Trauma theory imitates trauma; the theory itself is mimetically trapped in a repetition of the event. Indeed, this conception of trauma can spread outside its locus of origin and duplicate itself everywhere. Ultimately, all experience is seen as traumatic; and everyone becomes a victim (including the perpetrators).

## THE REPRESSION OF MEMORY

Another aspect of trauma theory needs to be discussed, before going on to a more general discussion of *mimesis*. There is a tendency in trauma therapy to focus on what has come to be called 'repressed memories.' These are understood to be memories that are not available to conscious recall, but which surface in the form of disguised symptoms. Superficially, this notion resembles the Freudian concept of repression, but a closer look shows some key differences.

For Freud, repression is carried out as a defensive measure by the ego when threatened with overwhelming anxiety. The anxiety comes from the guilt aroused by the impulse to commit an act prohibited by the conscience. The ego acts, in other words, under the spur of the superego, which serves (among other functions) as the supervising agency of the psyche that guards against the violation of internal norms. Since, in Freud's concept of 'psychic reality,' there is no psychically experienced difference between a wish and a deed, it is enough for the prohibited impulse to arise as a fantasy for the mechanism of repression to be set into operation. We guard against the anxiety aroused by the emergence of 'immoral' thoughts by banishing them from consciousness. For Freud, the energy of an impulse must be discharged in some manner. Therefore, if the fantasy is prohibited from awareness, it will re-emerge in the disguised form of the symptom.

Of course, not all anxiety-producing experiences are repressed. Realistic anxiety, which threatens the survival of the organism and which comes from the environment, is met by the ego with more-or-less appropriate defensive strategies carried out in full awareness. It is only internally generated anxiety that results in repression. But even then it is clear that not all prohibited impulses are banished from consciousness; indeed, we often feel guilty about our thoughts. The prohibited fantasy must threaten the very existence of the superego; it must, in fact, violate the basic norm which established that agency in the first place. In Freud's view, this is exactly what occurs. Since the superego arose as a consequence of the resolution of the Oedipus conflict, any Oedipal wishes threaten its very being. Therefore only these are kept from consciousness.

In other words, for Freud, 'repressed' memories are ultimately memories of Oedipal fantasies. They may indeed occur on the occasion of actual incestuous violations; contrary to what is sometimes asserted, Freud nowhere denied the reality of sexual abuse (though he did deny its universality). But what was significant for him were the fantasies that became aroused, either by the actual occurrence of the imagined events or by other, primarily constitutional, causes. Without these fantasies, no act of repression is necessary. This explains why some traumatic events are remembered and some are not (or rather, why some events become traumatic and others do not).

In Freud's later speculations on trauma, particularly after the horrors of the First World War, he focuses not so much on the repression of traumatic memories but on their tendency to recur in undistorted forms (e.g. nightmares) that produce conscious and overwhelming anxiety

(Freud 1990). This tendency seems to oppose the functioning of the pleasure principle, and accordingly must be attributed to a drive other than the libidinal one. Freud therefore postulates a death drive, representing a compulsion to repeat. This compulsion accounts for the re-emergence of painful memories in spite of the ego's tendency, assisted by the superego, to ward them off. What is remarkable here is that it is now the *memory* of the trauma that requires explanation for Freud, not its repression. If the traumatic memory is repressed, this can still be accounted for only within libidinal terms, by referring to the desire of the subject, even if that desire is unconscious.

In contemporary trauma theory, on the other hand, the notion of 'repressed memories' is quite different. In this model, the experience of a traumatic event is understood as unavailable to memory, because the event was itself experienced without any awareness, even unconscious awareness. This occurs in situations in which the event threatens the very survival of the individual, which can occur only when the event is so overwhelming that it is beyond the capacity of the ego to encompass it. The shock of the event is conceived of as so great that it tears the ego apart, separating experience and awareness. In fact, one could say that the trauma is not experienced at all, in so far as experience requires some form of awareness, conscious or not.

In its wish not to blame the victim, trauma theory is thus led to a notion of 'repression' that takes away all responsibility from the survivors, eliminating their capacity to respond. I repeat that I am not speaking here about responsibility for the trauma itself, which is never the fault of the victims, even if they have put themselves at risk. Within the framework of trauma theory, however, survivors cannot be responsible for their experience, since they cannot be said to have had the experience in the first place. That is to say, their experience lacked awareness – the most basic quality of experience.

From the perspective of contemporary trauma theory, an event is traumatic when it is so overwhelming to the subjects that they must split themselves off from all awareness. Memory of the event, normally a potential feature of all experience, is thereby prohibited. The experience cannot be integrated into the continuity of the temporal flow of the person's existence; it is discontinuous, a break in history which is interruptive, recurring again and again unless it is re-called in therapy. This therapeutic recollection can occur only as a repetition of the event, but this time with awareness. Thus the therapist seeks to 're-awaken' the memories and to enable the client to re-live them in the therapeutic situation, to experience them, it might be said, for the first time. The ability to 'testify' to one's history depends upon this previous re-enactment. And the testimony itself is understood to be the literal truth, just as the re-enactment is seen as a mimetic repetition in full awareness.

There are some curious consequences of this understanding. First, trauma is conceived in such a complete opposition to conscious experience that it becomes impossible to consistently understand how survivors of war or sexual abuse are able to remember their experiences at all. The logical conclusion would be that these experiences were not traumatizing for them, an insupportable conclusion. Second, if trauma is inaccessible to experience (except through its 'cure'), then all unwelcome feelings or actions can be explained as the result of previous trauma. There is a tendency in the field to see all symptoms of psychic disturbance, no matter how mild or common, as traumatic in their origin.

Moreover, one could say that, in a way, trauma victims are themselves victimized through this conception of trauma. Victims are seen as wholly passive, without will or impulse. In other words, they are treated in the same way that they were by the victimizer, as not fully human. This renders inconceivable an understanding of the resiliency of trauma victims, their capacity to respond to the event in a resourceful and creative manner.

## THE MIMESIS OF POIESIS

By undertaking this critique of the concept of *mimesis* within trauma therapy, I am not attempting to establish a theoretical position outside the mimetic field. Anti-mimesis, as we observed in the previous chapter, is as much trapped by its rival as *mimesis* is by itself. Anti-mimetic discourse is shadowed, haunted, by the ghost of the mimetic, which it vainly tries to dispel by opening wide the doors of consciousness. But there is nowhere to hide from one's shadow, one's ghost, one's spirit or *Geist* (particularly the spirit of one's time, the shadow cast by the *Zeit-Geist*).

How then to proceed? One way is to look more closely at the location in which *mimesis* first manifested itself. The origin of the concept of *mimesis*, as we have said, lies not in trauma but in the arts.

The *locus classicus* for our understanding of the term, again, is Plato's *Republic*, in which he distinguishes between philosophy, grounded in truth, and art, based on *mimesis* or imitation. Yet this opposition, which seems so clear in its presentation by Socrates, is actually undermined from within. In the first place, the very mode of philosophical inquiry, the dialogue form, is itself presented as the *mimesis* of an actual event, in which Socrates engaged in a conversation about the constitution of the just city. Moreover, Socrates' discourse in the dialogue is characterized not only by logical inquiry but also by the use of several poetic modes of *mimesis* (such as metaphor, image and story-telling), including the central allegory of the Cave, which is the imitation of the philosophical journey itself from seeming to being. Finally, the dialogue ends in a myth, a poetic form that is seen as the only adequate answer to the limits of philosophical knowledge, limits that are due to the embodiment of the soul. Philosophy is depicted in the *Phaedo* as having an essential connection with death (even as a 'rehearsal for death'); nevertheless, philosophical knowledge reaches its limit in the face of death and must give way to myth.

*Mimesis* is not only employed as a rhetorical strategy in the dialogues. It also partially forms the content of Platonic thought, in which the relationship of the particular things to the forms of true being is said to be one of 'imitation' (*mimesis*). The more usual Platonic term, it is true, is 'participation' (*methexis*); but the vexing question arises, among others, of how it is possible to recognize such participation if there is no 'resemblance' involved. In fact, Platonic thinking is mimetic through and through.

This mimetic quality should not be surprising if we recall the story that Plato's original intention was to become a tragic poet, and that it was only upon the occasion of a chance encounter with Socrates that he was motivated to give up the poetic vocation in favor of the philosophical one. The 'quarrel' between poetry and philosophy may itself be an instance of *mimesis*, it seems. There is a 'mimetic rivalry' between the two, to use a term of René Girard's (1977). (The question remains whether this rivalry could also be the basis of a mimetic friendship between them, as Nietzsche, for example, would prefer.)

Let us look again at the phenomenon of *mimesis* that shows itself through the Platonic critique. *Mimesis* is understood by him within the framework of *poiesis*, which we usually translate as 'poetry.' However, the Greeks used 'poetry' as a term designating all the arts, much as we use 'art' (or in German, *Kunst*) as the generic term. This seemingly casual linguistic difference reveals a great deal about the dominant characteristics of the two historical periods. To take the term for visual art, in contrast to the term for poetry, as the privileged mode of reference to the entire province of the arts, reveals a difference in sensory and cultural preference. What has been called the 'hegemony of vision' (Levin 1993) in our cultural discourse is in contrast to the leading role which the voice and its reception, speaking and listening, played for the Greeks (the other generic term for the arts, *mousike*, music, is clearly itself rooted in audition). Certainly every culture draws on all the sensory modalities. The Greeks themselves valued sight highly, as would any people bathed in Mediterranean light. Nevertheless, there is a way in which pre-Platonic Greece prized oral performance, whether in politics or the arts, that reveals an emphasis on audition in Greek culture as opposed to the emphasis on vision in our own. Although, for example, the Greeks valued physical beauty highly as a sign of excellence, the true mark of value for them was revealed in the ability to speak well. This accounts for the success of the Sophists, whose primary claim was to teach the art of argument in public discourse.

The predominance of visual metaphors in Plato – beginning with his central concept of *eidos* ('form' or 'idea'), which originally meant 'the visible aspect of what is,' and which came to mean for him, 'that which enables the thing to appear as it does, something only accessible to the eye of the mind' – signifies a change in the character of Greek culture. This change can also be understood as a shift from orality to literacy, as the predominance of spoken language gives way to that of a written one.

In fact, when Plato uses the term *poiesis*, he does not mean what we signify by our word 'poetry,' namely, a literary art. For Plato, as we have said, *poiesis* is primarily oral performance. Whether it is a question of the itinerant poets who traveled from court to court reciting their tales (as Homer was reputed to have done) or of the tragic dramas presented at the festivals, poetry is understood not just in terms of language but in terms of its actual performance. Moreover, the essence of poetry (at least as Plato presents it, in a way that indicates that this is common usage) is taken to be *mimesis*, not in the sense of imitation but rather in the sense of dramatic enactment.

The Platonic critique of *mimesis*, extended by him to all the arts, is based upon the common Greek understanding of the primacy of performance. When Plato discusses the poets in *The Republic*, for example, he distinguishes the narrative from the dramatic aspect of poetry. The poet who narrates an event, as in Homer's epic recitation, speaks about and re-presents the event's occurrence; he is in no way as reprehensible for Plato as the poet or actor in a drama who embodies the characters and therefore becomes that which he imitates. In the case of narrative, the danger of imitation is limited to a mis-representation of the event in question; it is a cognitive danger. But in the case of dramatic enactment, there is the actual making-present of that which does not exist; the danger therefore is ontological.

Dramatic *mimesis*, as we have noted, cannot be comprehended as the literal repetition of an action. Such 'literalism' is possible only with the introduction of writing. It is true that in oral cultures the story-teller presents his story not only as if it were about the way things were ('In the beginning...'), but also as if it were told in the way that it always has been. However, any ethnographic observer can testify to the variation in a single performer's repetitions, not to mention the differences in the way that different tellers tell the same tale and the different changes that the story itself undergoes over time. There is nothing less identical than oral performance, at least until the story is written down.

In the epic and tragic performances, there was certainly a text that was 'repeated.' But since the repetition itself was oral, not written, it always involved the media of the actor's body and voice, and, in the case of tragedy, of the particular character of the dramatic production. As we have said, no two productions of a text are the 'same,' in the sense of identical reproductions. Even the same show is different in its actual performance each night. Nevertheless there is repetition involved; it is the same text that is performed each time. No matter whose Hamlet it is, we expect the same melancholy Dane to appear. Even the rehearsal is an act of repetition (in French, 'rehearsal' is *répétition*): we practice the work over and over again.

Poetry, like all the arts, never involves a literal reproduction of its model. The limits of time and space, if nothing else, prevent that from happening. Moreover, not all aspects of an event can be presented, but only those that are significant, that reveal the essence of the story in question. That is why when Aristotle says that tragedy is the imitation of an action, he clearly means that what is 'imitated' is the 'form' of the action, that which enables it to be the action it is. And the 'imitation' is not seen by him as a 'representation' at a distance, but as a 'making-present' in the scene.

Drama, we could say, is the enactment of a story in the present, or in other words, the presentation of myth. The myth happens again, right here and now. It becomes present for us, not as something depicted as 'having been,' as it would be in a narrative mode, but as 'happening now,' before our eyes. This is not a magical act; the past action is not made present in its literal being. Rather it is given in a fictional, 'as if' mode: the action is presented as if it were present; it is the *mimesis* of the action, not its being.

There is a curious duality in *mimesis* that escapes Platonic dualism. Dramatic action both is and is not real. We know that no one dies on stage, but we are nonetheless affected by the imagined death. *Mimesis* is 'in between' being and non-being; it both is and is not. It possesses what we might call a 'virtual power,' an effect whose actuality depends upon fantasy.

This mixed ontological status of the mimetic cannot be caught within the logic of identity, which insists that something either is or is not itself (the basis of the principle of non-contradiction on which logical thinking depends). The true province of the mimetic is in the realm of play, in which we work hard, from childhood on, to create fictive worlds. No wonder we call dramatic performance a 'play,' in both English and German (*Spiel*), and performers 'players.'

This 'ludic' or playful quality of performance is so great that the mimetic relationship can be metaphorically reversed and the world itself seen as a stage with all its players on it (remembering that this is itself stated within a play). Truly, *homo ludens* (the human being as player) (Huizinga 1971) is a useful trope, as long as one remembers that we always play *at* something. *Mimesis* is not self-sufficient; it requires the non-mimetic for its referent. The alternative would be the world of simulacra that Jean-François Lyotard (1993, p.67) decried (though occasionally mimicking it himself). Post-modern discourse, in the practice of its critique of 'the metaphysics of presence,' is in fact playful through and through.


## DIONYSIAN *POIESIS*

What is it that is being played at in mimetic performance? What is at play in this event? Here I would like to go back to (i.e., 'repeat') the discourse of Nietzsche on Greek tragedy in *The Birth of Tragedy* (1967). Without claiming to do justice to this seminal work, I would like to retrieve from it the central thought that continues to recur in Nietzsche's writing, that of the Dionysian, and see to what extent this thought can be understood within the framework of *poiesis*.

As is well known, Nietzsche began his academic career as a philologist, a student of Greek language and literature. What is characteristic of him as one who recommends self-overcoming is that *The Birth of Tragedy* is an attack, in part, upon the philological or literary reading of Greek tragedy. For the literary scholars, the tragic dramas were texts, written pieces whose distinguishing characteristic was the exquisite beauty of their ordered poetic language. This interpretation, of course, fit the overall image in the German world of classic Attic culture as having a 'harmonious' and 'sun-filled' character. The cultivation of Greek 'serenity' was thus seen as an ideal for cultural development (*Bildung*).

For Nietzsche, however, tragedy is first and foremost not a literary event but a dramatic one. Tragic drama is to be performed, not read. This changes our relation to the dramas from one of historical scholarship to a living encounter in the present. The encounter takes place, one might say, in Nietzsche's imagination; but the power of his imaginative vision is such that the tragic spirit (the 'ghost' of tragedy) becomes alive in his text. Nietzsche not only writes about tragedy; he writes tragically. Reading his text, then, should be done in the way one is present at a performance, transported within a fictive mode, not distanced from it in a reflective one. (The complaints that Nietzsche's account is historically inaccurate, however valid, thereby miss the point.)

In *The Birth of Tragedy*, Nietzsche is thinking like a poet. In this sense he accomplishes, at least in part, the task at which Socrates failed and which was left for future thinkers: to become a 'music-playing' philosopher. We could even say that Nietzsche has been infected by the spirit of tragedy; its contagious quality has taken him over; his text is, in other words, mimetically constituted. Perhaps it is indeed an example of mimetic friendship, in contradistinction to Girard's mimetic rivalry in which one of the rivals must destroy the other. The ancient quarrel between poetry and philosophy is here taken up in a non-exclusionary way.

This procedure is in fact consistent with one of Nietzsche's most important insights into Greek culture: the predominance of the *agon* or contest (Nietzsche 2007). In Nietzsche's view, all value is measured within an agonistic framework for the Greeks, whether it be the competition of the Olympic games, the discourses in the law courts or the performance of tragedy itself. The tragic dramas, which were presented at festivals honoring the god Dionysos, were in fact entered into competition in an attempt to win the prize that led to the attainment of the laurel wreath, a sign of the favor of the god.

In Nietzsche's agonistic thinking, we discern an alternative to the mimetic violence that Girard sees everywhere. For Nietzsche and, as he saw it, for Greek culture as a whole, excellence depends not only on victory but also on the strength of the opponent. My excellence, therefore, depends upon that of my competitor's. Indeed, one could say that I have an ethical obligation to strengthen him in order to help him to compete at his best and thus, if I win, to increase my own glory in the sight of the gods. A victory in the style of American football (measured by the magnitude of the disparity of the final score) or modern warfare (measured by the disparity of lives lost) would be considered a disgrace.

For this reason, Nietzsche's later genealogical critique of morality ends with an agonistic self-overcoming, a victory over himself as a philosopher. Recall that for Nietzsche, in replacing the 'master' values of sensuality and enjoyment, the self-denial that Christianity commands produces a human being weakened of its essential powers. However it is not only the ascetic priest who is 'weak' in Nietzsche's eyes, but also the 'blond beast' of the master race, in so far as the latter's dominance is achieved at the expense of less powerful groups. In fact, the ascetic priest has won a greater victory, since his opponents were the rich and powerful of the world. Ultimately, for Nietzsche, to overcome the spirit of asceticism would mean to overcome it in oneself. The concept of 'truth,' the final victory of asceticism in the form of science and knowledge, must itself, in Nietzsche's view, be struggled against. The philosopher must go beyond his love of truth. He must, that is, be cruel towards his own cruelty; he must overcome himself. And to achieve this he needs the help of his ancient competitor, the poet.

Nietzsche's poetic thinking is nowhere more evident in his early work than in his depiction of Apollo and Dionysos. These are, it should be noted, presented as images rather than concepts, and this helps Nietzsche avoid the polarized oppositions to which abstract conceptions might otherwise lead. Apollo is not only 'form' and Dionysos 'energy,' in the manner of Schopenhauer's (ultimately Kant's) distinction between representation and will. Rather, Apollo and Dionysos are mythical beings, whose stories (and the rituals in which they are enacted) enable Nietzsche to think differently than if they were concepts in philosophical discourse.

The Dionysian element in tragic drama, for Nietzsche, is present in the chorus, whose music and dance resemble that of the revelers in the rites of their god. Seeing the tragic drama from a performative perspective not only enables Nietzsche to explain the role of the chorus (which is obscure from a literary point of view), but also allows him to re-cast the drama in a mode resembling that of Dionysian ritual, as a celebration of the life and death of the god. Dionysos is not only the god of revelry, of the vine, of collective celebration and laughter. He is also the dying god, torn apart in the spring, only to await his re-memberance in the autumn harvest (Dionysos is thus the embodiment of 'dissemination'). His followers mourn his death in order to celebrate his re-birth and the gifts that this brings. The wildness of Dionysian revelry is the orgiastic coming of new life from the grave of the dead.

Dionysos, we might even say, is the god of life, where life is understood as containing death within its orbit (the task, as Rilke saw it, of the lyric poet). Dionysos celebrates death-in-life and life-in-death. He is torn apart and fragmented but also re-membered, put together again. His funeral is his wake, his a-wakening, his passing and his coming. He is the embodiment of passage, of coming-into-being and passing away. Tragedy, then, is the performance of the Dionysian, the acceptance and affirmation of the Dionysian within the domain of *poiesis*. Apollo here acts as a friend to Dionysos, giving him the measure which poetic language brings. In the tragic performances at the festivals, Dionysos is in fact brought within the city walls. He is honored and given his rightful place. In return he brings his gifts of celebration and renewed vitality. A city without Dionysos is a city without life.

This is one way of understanding Euripides' *Bacchae*. Pentheus, the ruler of Thebes, acts according to the principles of Plato in *The Republic*: in his concern for civic order he refuses to recognize his kinship with Dionysos, and attempts to prevent him from entering the city. But Dionysos cannot be denied; he 'returns' in terrible form to lead Pentheus to his own destruction at the hands of the one who gave him birth, his mother, Agave. In trying to eliminate disorder, Pentheus ensures that chaos will result.

Note that the *Bacchae*, for all its references to ritual, is a play, not a ritual enactment. It is *as if* the god were present in the theater. The fact that pregnant women were said to have miscarried at its performance is no evidence that the show was not understood as dramatic performance. We are speaking here not of Dionysian ritual enacted outside the city walls (outside, that is, of the domain of culture), but of a 'Dionysian *poiesis*,' a welcoming of the anarchic energy of life in its coming and passing within the human (i.e. cultural) world.

Dionysos, then, presents two faces: the joy-affirming, celebratory appearance of life, and the destructive, fury-bearing manifestation of death. We might think that this duality of the 'god of many masks' (as he was called by the Greeks) could be understood as an opposition that is structured by our reception – if we welcome the god, he will bring new life; if we deny him, he will return, wreaking havoc and destruction, leaving death and mourning in his wake. To some extent this seems to be the way in which tragic drama presents it. But Nietzsche rejects such an 'optimistic' view of life. To him, Dionysos is the passing that brings both life and death. We cannot therefore 'Choose life!' in the sense of the Biblical injunction. In the tragic vision, to choose life is also to choose death. In fact it is the attempt to choose life without also accepting death that leads to chaos and destruction. We cannot embrace life without also embracing death.

To say all this is to return, in Nietzsche's eyes, to the Greek tragic wisdom which states that life is suffering, without, at the same time, trying to escape that suffering through a Schopenhauerian abnegation of the will. It is a 'pessimism of the strong,' which enables us to look the abyss in the face and not only to survive but also to live life to the fullest – to be able, in other words, to laugh. The 'spirit of seriousness' which permeates our culture can be overcome for Nietzsche only by the deep laughter which comes from knowing that one is dancing on the abyss, that there is no foundation which could exist to redeem our suffering.

The myth of the eternal return is, for Nietzsche, the highest test of our ability to affirm life. It calls on us to accept time not only for what is coming (a 'salvational' view) but also for what has been, to be willing to re-member every moment, not just the privileged ones, and say, in the words of Faust, 'Stay, thou art fair!' Here Nietzsche's 'will-to-power' stands revealed as the highest form of what Heidegger (1969) called *Gelassenheit* ('releasement' or 'letting-be'), the acceptance of Being as time. Dionysos, in fact, is the figure of time, time passing and time coming. Time comes again and again (which means it passes again and again). In its coming, therefore, it repeats itself. Time is repetition. But each time, time is 'different'; it is the time after and the time before. Time 'spaces' itself. Time is timing, *rhuthmos* (a measured movement, rhythm). It interrupts itself to repeat itself again. It beats itself out. For Aristotle (1961), time is the measure of movement, because time is movement in measure, the repetitive figure of passage and advent. Time, we might even say, 'mimetizes' itself; its passing is a self-resemblance which comes again and again. Temporality is mimetic.

This explains the Platonic resistance to *mimesis*. True being, for Plato, is outside of time (although even Plato cannot help wondering whether the Forms are without movement and life). Self-identity is possible only in an a-temporal realm. The death for which the Platonic philosopher longs is the escape from the self-diremption of time, (its non-coincidence with itself) not the acceptance of passing. This death will be like Parmenides' account of the way of truth: one, eternal, self-identical. All dialectic, for Plato, aims at self-abolition in the timeless intuition of eternal truth.

Poietic *mimesis*, on the other hand, is of this world. Its play of resemblance welcomes change, the creation and destruction of form. *Poiesis* knows that nothing lasts; and it celebrates this passing by showing its glorious manifestation. Its most permanent victory lies in the acceptance of its own transitoriness. All performance ultimately enacts the tragi-comedy, *panta rhei* (everything flows, as Heraclitus reputedly said).

## *POIESIS* AND POST-MODERNITY

What then is the truth of those who criticize *mimesis*? There is indeed a destructive *mimesis* which lies at the heart of trauma, war and human suffering. For René Girard, this destructiveness of *mimesis* consists in the principle of disorder which tears communities apart, unless they be appeased by the creation of the scapegoat who will be blamed for the chaos resulting from mimetic rivalry (Girard 1977). *Mimesis*, for Girard, appears primarily in its destructive form; it is only in his later thinking that an explicitly positive manifestation of *mimesis* is thematized: as the imitation of Christ (*imitatio Christi*). For Girard (2003), Christ breaks the cycle of mimetic rivalry by liberating us from the tyranny of time.

By taking on our sins in a willing sacrifice, he overcomes historical repetition and offers us eternal bliss.

The difficulty with Girard's view is not only that one must become a believing Christian to accept it (which tends to make him see all critics as unwitting agents of Satan), but also that it fails to find a this-worldly principle of *mimesis* as a creative power. In fact, Girard understands the mimetic problem as irresolvable in human history. For him, there is no escape from the violence of mimetic rivalry in this world; it is necessary to have a perspective that transcends time to accomplish this. Girard's thinking, therefore, seems to me to remain trapped within the 'metaphysics of presence' that post-modern thought has so strongly criticized.

The perspective I am presenting here, on the other hand, is a kind of modified post-modernism or, perhaps, an anticipation of what might come after post-modernism. Post-modernism is philosophy traumatized by history. Its opposition to philosophies of identity is not arbitrary, but stems from its insight into the consequences of totalizing forms, whether political or theoretical. The modernist project of totalization is dead; it survives for post-modernism only in the mode of globalization, identity under the sign of the logo.

To some extent the post-modernist project has a mimetic relationship to the failure of modernity; post-modernism enacts fragmentation as if it were the truth. Its celebration of the simulacrum as a strategy for over-coming modernity leaves post-modernism open to the charge of becoming part of what it seeks to go beyond. What it fails to remember is that *mimesis* is always repetition with a difference, a re-play that transforms what it resembles. The Dionysian spirit is struggling to emerge in the discourse of post-modernism. But we must remember that Dionysos is not only a figure of fragmentation; he is also in-gathering, conception, the re-membering of history that gives it new life without claiming that its suffering is at an end. Dionysos is a child playing in the ruins of time; he builds and destroys, leads us to mourn and to celebrate. We cannot celebrate unless we mourn; but we cannot truly mourn unless our mourning awakens us again. 'Only in the realm of Praising should Lament walk,' Rilke (1984b, p.237) tells us, while warning that only a god can bring together the worlds of life and death. As for us, he says, 'Our mind is split' (Rilke 1984b, p.231). Yet the Orphic poet can bring this Dionysian spirit to life, restoring it to its proper place in the world through the invocation of the poem, making it present therein even as he knows it is absent from his own life.

What accounts for violence, then, if it is not the mimetic *per se*? I would venture to say that violence proceeds from the denial of the Dionysian, from the disavowal of difference, in other words from the refusal to accept time. Violence refuses the difference of the other, and of the other in the self. It insists upon self-identity, not resemblance or likeness. 'You must be me or you have no right to exist,' is its motto. The destructive chaos of violence is a denial of the chaotic creativity of life; it is an attempt to impose order without change or difference.

Trauma, then, as the result of violence, is the experience of being negated in one's essential difference, not only one's different race, nation or gender, but also ultimately the difference which pertains to one's own existence itself. I am not the same as you; but neither am I other than you. I resemble you in existing; you can neither own nor disown me. To attempt either is to commit violence upon our resemblance. We do not have to destroy each other in order to have the right to exist; nor do we have to join together only by substituting a third whom we will destroy together. Rather, our rivalry can take place under the sign of friendship. We can play together and celebrate our differences; but first we must re-member what we have done to each other and vow not to repeat our past. The slogan 'Never again!' can thus be a motto for overcoming violence, but not if it means 'You will never do that to me again; I will kill you first so that you do not.' Rather, 'Never again' must mean 'I will never do again what they have done to me. I will remember my own suffering in order to be sure not to inflict it upon others.' How can we stop repeating the past? By doing it again differently, by honoring our differences, by re-membering difference itself, gathering it together into new life.

History repeats itself. We might indeed paraphrase Marx and say, 'History repeats itself, first as tragedy, then as trauma.' The figure of the victim of trauma has replaced that of the hero of tragedy as the emblem of human suffering. There is some justification for this change, as the discourse of trauma honors the suffering of those whose fates were in no way a consequence of their own choice. But the tragic hero as well was also not responsible for his act; clearly, the gods had ordained his doom without his will. Tragedy reminds us of the responsibility of the hero *to* his fate. Oedipus is unable to prevent the fulfillment of the prophecy that leads to his destruction, but he is able to accept it, and ultimately even to find the blessing that it brings.

In our times, it is much harder for us to see the blessing in suffering. Is there anything that can justify the horror of the Holocaust or other contemporary modes of mass death? Is the *mimesis* of a Dionysian *poiesis* strong enough to find after this any cause for celebration? Post-Holocaust *poiesis* has necessarily been led to search beyond the 'affirmative character of culture' (Marcuse 1969) to invent forms which enable us to 'write the disaster' (Blanchot 1995) without thereby overcoming it by an act of affirmation. The only cultural act, for example, which the West brought that was meaningful to the besieged and tormented inhabitants of Sarajevo was Susan Sontag's production of *Waiting for Godot*. In that tragi-comedy, no *deus ex machina* enters from the wings. Godot will never come, and the two tramps know this full well. Nevertheless they continue to wait. And while waiting, they do the only thing they can to 'pass the time': they play. For the war-traumatized citizenry, *Waiting for Godot was* Sarajevo. The play was a *mimesis* of their own reality, waiting for an intervention that would never come. The drama offered no resolution of their dilemma, only the 'pleasure' of recognition that resemblance brings, the bitter irony of waiting for a god who will never arrive.

A post-Holocaust *poiesis* must reject any hope that cannot be found in finitude itself. There is no god that can save us from history, only the god of history itself, the god of departure and arrival. We know that time will go on coming and overcoming. Can we be in time with it? Can we find its measure? The figure of Dionysos reminds us that suffering and celebration can find their time. Dionysian *poiesis* enacts the *mimesis* of time. It is a performance of healing that honors the dead and prepares the way for the living. Only in this way can we re-member what we have been.

## *POIESIS*, CATHARSIS AND THE END OF THERAPY

What are the implications of these reflections for therapeutic treatment? It would be a mistake to take them as a rationale for the minimization of suffering. On the contrary, it seems to me that a perspective based on a Dionysian conception of *poiesis* would recognize the universality of suffering inherent in the finitude of our existence. Trauma does not take place outside the orbit of human experience. *Pathos* or suffering belongs to our very being; in a sense, we might say that existence *is* trauma, the ec-static suffering of time. We must, therefore, situate specifically 'traumatic' events within the context of finite being. Trauma theory tends to understand trauma as a foreign body entering a trauma-free being from without; it thus implies a vision of human being as essentially innocent and free from suffering. If we hold to this view, we would run the risk of therapeutic messianism. Overcoming trauma would then mean restoring primeval innocence, seen as a 'natural' condition. Ultimately, contemporary trauma theory implies that it is culture that is the cause of trauma. Within its framework, to heal the trauma victim would be to restore her to her natural state of innocence.

From the standpoint of a Dionysian *poiesis*, however, healing must be understood differently. Again, it may help us if we return to another Greek word, one often used by trauma therapists themselves: *catharsis*. As we noted, the most common use of the term stems from one of its significations, the medical meaning of expelling a toxic substance from the body. Thus trauma therapy considers its task to be the elimination of the trauma through a mimetic repetition of the original event. Trauma is then conceived of as a foreign body which must be expelled to restore health. But catharsis, in its ritual use, also originally had the sense of 'purification.' To purify something in this sense is not to purge it of impurities but to convert these toxic qualities into beneficial ones. Indeed it could be said that the poison consists in the attempt to expel it, to refuse to see it as a gift that can confer a blessing. If the gift is also the poison, as Derrida tells us (and as the German word for poison, *Gift*, indicates), it is also true that the poison may be the gift (Derrida 1981). This is not the gift of redemption but the gift of death, which is accepted only through rites of mourning and celebration. It is in this sense that I would understand Aristotle's statement that the *mimesis* of *poiesis* brings *catharsis*.

The conception, in trauma therapy, of *catharsis* as the product of a literal repetition of the traumatic event cannot account for this beneficial effect. 'Repetition' repeats itself; there is a tendency for a 'cathartic' experience to be repeated over and over again without result. Rather, what is necessary is to recognize that the trauma 'belongs' to me. Whatever my responsibility in bringing it about, it is now mine, which means that it is subject to the character of my experience as a human being – in fact, it is made possible by this character. I cannot rid myself of it; it is not possible for me to return to an earlier pre-traumatized state of being, since the condition of the possibility of trauma is inherent in my being itself.

What I can do is purify the trauma by affirming it through an act of *poiesis*. That is to say, I can 'repeat it differently' by shaping it in another form. My remembering, then, will be at the same time a kind of imagining; I will see through the event to its possibilities. *Poiesis* within a therapeutic context means that my suffering is not eliminated, but given meaning and value through a transformative act of poetic imagination. This is not the auto-production of a transcendental subject, a being outside of the world. Rather, it is achieved through the *Gelassenheit* of acceptance, in which is revealed a faith that even without transcendence a gift will be received.

Therapy has reached its end with trauma. For this end to be a beginning, we must find the forms adequate to suffering in our time. In its encounter with *poiesis*, therapy is led out of the consulting room and into the world. Social suffering can be met only by a practice of communal mourning and celebration. We recall that Dionysos is the god of the community; he gathers us together in our conception, our birth. This is not the self-identity of the members of a collectivity; each of us 'differs' from the other. But in our being-in-common (Nancy 2000, p.55), we can recognize our suffering and our hope.

*Poiesis* is always possible. This is the groundless hope of a Dionysian philosophy, that even in an abyssal world, it is still possible to sing. The songs themselves may carry the silence of the void. They may come in the pause between, the caesura, the breath-turn, but in this moment something will emerge, a birth to presence (Nancy 1993). Let us repeat our history and thereby prepare ourselves for what is to come.

# Part II
# Chaos into Form

5

# Order and Chaos in
# Therapy and the Arts

## *An Encounter*

The experience of trauma is often understood as one in which chaos is introduced into the life of an individual or community. How can we understand the role which chaos plays in therapy and the arts? In this chapter, I try to deepen the question through an encounter with Rudolf Arnheim, the distinguished psychologist whose work on the psychology of art was based on the pre-eminence of the art-work as an ordered whole. Arnheim was one of the great psychologists of art of the twentieth century, the one who most clearly envisioned the arts as ways of overcoming the chaotic events of that historical period.

Arnheim described his own life as having taken place 'in the company of the century' (1992). Born in the early 1900s, he witnessed the chaos and disorder of a turbulent epoch. At the same time, he continually affirmed the need for order, balance and structure in human life and art. This chapter will encounter Arnheim's thinking in terms of the opposition between chaos and order. In particular, we will ask whether Arnheim's psychology of art can serve as a framework for understanding the theory and practice of the creative and expressive arts therapies today. Can Arnheim's thinking, with its emphasis on form and structure, contain the chaos of our own experience as artists and therapists? Only an answer to this question can establish the relevance of his writings for our own work.

At the same time, an encounter with Arnheim puts our own thinking into question. Are we missing an essential dimension of art-making when we emphasize spontaneity over formal constraints? Is the aesthetic

experience of the work neglected in the contemporary dominance of
process? Is aesthetic perception at least as important as the usual goal
of self-expression? And, finally, do we overlook the role of order and
structure by focusing on the disorderly and the chaotic in the work of
clients or patients?

An encounter with Arnheim thus begins a process of mutual
questioning, in which the presuppositions of both discourses become
apparent. This process is often referred to as a hermeneutic circle, a
circle of interpretation. In an authentic act of interpretation, not only
what is interpreted comes into question, but also the position of the
interpreter becomes questionable. Ultimately, the question becomes not
so much what do we have to say about Arnheim's work as, what can this
work teach us about ourselves?

Born in Berlin to a secular, assimilated Jewish family, Rudolf
Arnheim passed his early years in the twilight of the German Empire.
It was, in his words, 'an age of innocence. Around us the world seemed
still at peace' (1992, p.236). After the shock of the First World War, the
Weimar Republic ushered in a creative but uncertain epoch. Arnheim
talks about a 'profound sense of unreliability...a sense of not being
able to trust the foundations of our habitat' (1992, p.237). Reassurance
came for him from the study of the arts and the emerging science of
Gestalt psychology. In both areas he found an antidote to the prevailing
disorder:

> Great painting and sculpture as well as great architecture
> offered the perfection of harmony and order indispensable as a
> framework of reference by which to judge the precarious insuf-
> ficiencies of the world surrounding me. Gestalt psychology was
> equally committed to the striving of organized forces toward a
> goal state of equilibrium, clarity and simplicity. (1992, p.238)

The history of art and the science of psychology, then, became the
dual sources of Arnheim's subsequent writings. Drawing from both
traditions, he produced an impressive collection of systematic works, as
well as numerous essays that show an increasing mastery of these two
fields and an ability to apply their principles to other areas of human
experience and thought. This chapter will not provide an overall review
of his work, but, rather, will attempt to focus on his search for order
in psychology and the arts – a search which, it seems to me, is the
dominant theme of his work.

Already in *Film as Art* (1957), published in Germany in 1932, Arnheim emphasized the priority of order in art and life: '...a population constantly exposed to chaotic sights and sounds is gravely handicapped in finding its way. When the eyes and ears are prevented from perceiving meaningful order, they can only react to the brutal signals of immediate satisfaction' (p.6). As a consequence, Arnheim claimed, the introduction of sound into film, by breaking the structural unity of the visual image, created a 'radical artistic impoverishment' (p.230). The talking picture is a hybrid form that fails to achieve the necessary unit of the work of art.

But it is not until the appearance of Arnheim's masterwork, *Art and Visual Perception,* in 1954, that the full outlines of his theory became clear. In this work (extensively revised in 1974), Arnheim provided a systematic application of the principles of Gestalt psychology to the study of visual perception and the arts (with a special focus on, but not limited to, the arts of painting and sculpture). In order to understand Arnheim's accomplishment here, it is necessary to recall the original project of the Gestalt psychologists, formulated in Germany in the early decades of the twentieth century.

Up to that point, psychological research into perception had been dominated by the theory of association, according to which the discrete data of the senses are unified by the intellect according to rules of contiguity and resemblance. In this traditional view, if I am able to recognize the objects about me, it is because the shapes and colors of the visual world, meaningless in themselves, are tied together by the repetition of innumerable experiences. By recalling experiences that were similar, or that occurred next to each other in space or time, the intellect is able to give form and order to the meaningless chaos of the senses. Thus, for associationist theory, the senses by themselves are dumb; they contain nothing except raw data that must be processed by the faculty of judgment into meaningful forms.

Gestalt psychology showed that this theory not only denigrated perception, but that it also made the practice of art unintelligible. If the visual artist works with meaningless shapes and colors, then meaning can only reside in a semantic content that is superimposed on the work. The visual shape of the work would then be the arbitrary carrier of a meaning derived from a linguistically centered tradition. Within a framework based on the psychology of association, art is understood to use the visual image as an inadequate representation for thought; it is, therefore, suitable only for those incapable of pure conceptual thinking.

The discoveries of the early Gestalt psychologists Köhler, Koffka and Wertheimer revealed the inadequacy of associationist psychology. The Gestaltists conducted laboratory experiments in perceptual variation that showed that perception is always structured. Gestalt or form is basic to the perceptual act, not imposed by the intellect upon the chaos of sense-perception.

By showing that a shape is always affected by its context, for example, Gestalt psychology revealed the dependence of the parts upon the whole. A sense datum is never an isolated independent entity; it always occurs within a context that modifies its values according to its relationships with other entities. Moreover, not only does the whole determine the parts, but also the parts constitute the whole; if there is a variation of a sub-group, the entire structure will be modified. This mutual dependence of parts and whole revealed an organic unity in the field of perception. Holism, for the Gestaltists, is not a philosophy; it is the empirical condition for the experience of any perception whatsoever.

Arnheim shows that this confidence in the structural unity of the perceptual field has radical consequences for the understanding of vision as well as of art. Meaningful forms are already present in the visual field before any act of judgment, but these structures are not passively received by the organism. Rather, the organism conducts a formative structuring of its environment as a creative act. 'Far from being a mechanical recording of sensory elements, vision proved to be a creative apprehension of reality – imaginative, inventive, shrewd and beautiful' (1954/1974, p.5). The phenomenal world around us is characterized by meaningful relationships; vision is a comprehension of that world in its essential features. As Arnheim put it, 'eyesight is insight' (1974 [1954], p.46).

Moreover, the structures that characterize vision are not static and inert presences; rather, they are dynamic tendencies. 'Visual experience is dynamic'; it is characterized by 'an interplay of directed tensions' (1974 [1954], p.46). Shapes and colors combine in ways that affect each other; they show a tendency to move in a certain direction depending upon the context. Percepts interact in order to form dynamic wholes. The visual world is alive with meaning and form.

The implications for art of Arnheim's Gestalt analysis of visual perception are clear. In the first place, there is a continuity between art and vision that makes artistic practice comprehensible. If vision itself is creative, then artists are only explicitly doing what is implicit in every perceptual act: they shape the environment in a creative and meaningful way in accordance with certain basic principles of perception. Art is not a mystical capacity remote from everyday experience. In a sense, we are all artists by virtue of being embodied in the sensible world. The artist merely makes this common heritage explicit.

Second, the presence of structure in the very act of perception implies that forms have meaning. At the same time, meaning can only be embodied in forms that express it in a suitable manner. The forms of art are not accidental and extrinsic to the meaning of the work; rather, they are the media that carry the meaning. An art-work is thus the creation of an expressive form that directly conveys a meaning through sensible experience. Conventional and traditional meanings or symbols find their place in the work only through the sensible forms themselves; the latter carry these meanings in a more or less appropriate way.

Arnheim's analysis of art is based upon a rehabilitation of the senses. The meaning of the work appears through sense-experience; we see it directly. Just as we see the world as a field of directed forces, so we immediately see the work as a whole in all the dynamic interplay of its parts. The work reveals itself to the senses; its meaning is carried by the play of sensible forms within it.

Furthermore, the emphasis on sensible form in Arnheim's work makes possible an understanding of modern art. If forms carry meaning directly, then it is not necessary for representational images to bring significance to the work. In fact, Arnheim claims, the preference for realistic representation is a relatively new and 'unnatural' way of making art. We have to be taught to see realistic art; it is by no means a direct expression of our human nature.

The abstractions of modernist art, for Arnheim, carry the deepest spiritual values in a direct and unmediated way. The paintings of Mondrian, for example, make perfect sense when understood within this framework. Abstract shapes and colors convey meaning in a world in which traditional symbols are without significance. Modernist abstraction thus takes us back to the source of art-making in the creativity of visual perception.

In Arnheim's view, the power of a work of art comes from its creation of order and balance. This emphasis on balance is particularly appropriate to our encounter with Arnheim's work. What, after all, does he mean by a structure? A structure, for him, consists in the balance of an interplay of forces. In general, Arnheim, following the principles of Gestalt psychology, sees perception as tending toward an equilibrium that reduces tension in the phenomenal field. Tension reduction is a fundamental goal of the organism. This perceptual tendency is expressed in what Arnheim calls the 'law of simplicity,' the tendency of any perceived structure to express itself in the simplest form possible.

Balance in the work of art, then, is achieved by following the law of simplicity so that the forces depicted find a satisfactory equilibrium. At the same time, Arnheim is clear that simplicity alone is not the goal either for the organism or for the artist. If it were, the simplest form would be the most satisfying. In fact, the organism also obeys a counter-tendency toward vitality and enhancement of its level of energy. This goal is achieved perceptually by the experience of tension and complexity in the environment. As Arnheim put it in the first edition of *Art and Visual Perception*, 'the most characteristic feature of the organism is its revolt against what the physicist calls the increase of entropy…The processes of growth and the striving for vital aims are most typically organic' (1974 [1954], p.359).

Accordingly, the work of art distinguishes itself not so much by its simplicity as by its ability to encompass the highest levels of tension and complexity within the simplest possible form. Modernist art may look simple, but in fact a perceptual analysis of the visual forms of a work reveals that its simplicity is limited by the tension and complexity needed for the expression of a particular theme. It is in fact the theme or meaning of the work that determines its level of simplicity or complexity. A complex theme demands the simplest structure capable of containing its complexity; anything simpler would be inappropriate for the expression of the theme.

What interests us particularly in Arnheim's argument here is his attempt to account for this counter-tendency to the principle of simplicity. Although it is mentioned in the writings of other Gestalt psychologists, Arnheim is, I believe, the first of them to emphasize this principle of complexity. Perhaps he is able to do so because of his focus on the structure of the work of art, a structure impossible to comprehend in terms of simplicity alone.

In the second edition (1974) of *Art and Visual Perception,* Arnheim called the tendency to complexity an 'anabolic or constructive tendency, the creation of a structural theme. This structural theme constitutes what the mind is about, what it is after' (p.411) In a short monograph published in 1971, *Entropy and Art: An Essay on Disorder and Order,* Arnheim elaborated on this notion. The structural theme, he states, 'introduces and maintains tension. In the arts the theme represents what the work "is about"' (Arnheim 1971, p.52). The anabolic tendency satisfies a 'need for complexity' that is basic to our humanity but is perhaps particularly strong in creative personalities. A structural theme contains a message about the relationship between human beings and their world. Order itself is not enough: 'What is ultimately required is that this order reflect a genuine, true profound view of life' (Arnheim 1971, p.51).

In *Entropy and Art,* Arnheim (1971) discussed the second law of thermodynamics, the principle of entropy, to draw certain conclusions about the significance of order in art. In fact, the argument of the book is that this principle, according to which the amount of entropy in the universe tends to increase to an absolute state, should not be interpreted to reflect a fundamental preference of the universe for disorder and thereby to justify chaos as a model for artistic practice. Rather, in Arnheim's view, the dissipation of energy envisioned by the increase in entropy results not in chaos but in the simplest possible form of order, a side-by-side homogenous similarity of elements. This is not chaos but mere orderliness without complexity.

Chaos, on the other hand, is produced by what Arnheim called the 'catabolic effect,' a category that comprises 'all sorts of agents and events that act in an unpredictable, disorderly fashion and have in common the fact that they all grind things to pieces' (1971, p.28). Catabolic destruction produces chaotic disorder. It destroys structures and thereby also the meanings that they express. In so far as art is the creation of dynamic structures, catabolism is anti-art.

Anabolism and catabolism are variations on the fundamental tendency of an organism to change or transform itself (i.e., 'metabolism' – from the Greek, *metabole,* to change). Anabolism is, literally, to change 'up' or in a constructive direction; catabolism is to change 'down' or destructively. Building-up and breaking-down are two fundamental ways of bringing about change. Their action has the effect of increasing or decreasing complexity, respectively.

Thus, in addition to the aforementioned tendency toward simplicity that counteracts complexity, there is also the possibility of the breaking-up of complex wholes through destructive disintegration. Catabolism breaks up complex structures into chaotic, disorderly parts. We note that Arnheim described this process as an 'effect' rather than a 'tendency,' as in the anabolic case. This is because he sees the constructive building up of complex systems of order as an inherent human drive. Break-down, on the other hand, is something that happens 'from without'; it represents pathology in the organism and in cultural life. Therefore catabolism is not intrinsic to human existence; it is an accidental process that interferes with the essential tendency toward order.

Within this framework, then, contemporary tendencies in art toward chaos and disorder are seen by Arnheim as a degradation of our essential humanity. He objects to the accepting of 'disorder in the work of an artist as an interpretation of disorder when we recognize it as a mere addition to it' (1971, p.54). We should note that Arnheim is not rejecting the depiction of disorder; he is far from calling for a seamless, harmonious art without tension or complexity. But he demands that the disorder expressed in the work not be the product of a disorderly work itself.

Catabolic tendencies in art are, for him, a symptom of cultural breakdown; they reflect the latter without surmounting it. Chance, accident and randomness in the creation of art-works represent 'the pleasures of chaos' rather than the responsibilities of art. 'Disintegration and excessive tension reduction must be attributed to the absence or impotence of articulate structure. It is a pathological condition' (Arnheim 1971, p.55).

Arnheim does acknowledge the positive goal of what we might call 'catabolic art': the 'almost desperate need to wrest order from a chaotic environment' (1971, p.55). He also acknowledges the value of such art as symptomatic of the cultural chaos in which the contemporary artist and audience live. But, at the same time, he resists the tendency in present-day art-making toward break-down and disorder; for him, this tendency transcends the limits of art in the direction of anti-art.

Arnheim returned to the theme of order and disorder in *The Dynamics of Architectural Form*, published in 1977. Here he again rejected the possibility of an art based on disorder, criticizing in particular Robert Venturi's book, *Complexity and Contradiction in Architecture* (1966). Arnheim cited approvingly Venturi's emphasis on tension and complexity in the history of architecture, in opposition to the sometimes enforced simplicities and geometric regularities of modernist architectural style. This emphasis fits in well with Arnheim's own recognition of complexity as a basic human tendency. At the same time, however, he rejected Venturi's notion that architectural complexity can be understood as a form of contradiction. Contradiction, for Arnheim, is 'an offense against order. It is a mistake committed out of ignorance or oversight or for a misguided purpose' (Arnheim 1977, p.163). Such contradiction prevents an object from carrying out its purpose; and, because architecture is above all else a functional art, contradiction has no place in architectural design.

Arnheim's criticisms here are particularly significant given the development of architecture in recent decades. Post-modern architecture, with its emphasis on the discordant combination of different stylistic impulses and the consequent lack of an overall unity of design, represents a challenge to Arnheim's aesthetic standards. Whereas his earlier championing of the abstractions of modernism in opposition to the demands of traditional realism seemed to put him in accordance with the development of contemporary art, his insistence on the primacy of order made it difficult for him to acknowledge the value of any art that deliberately seeks out the disorderly and tries not simply to master but to embody it.

Of course, Arnheim might argue that the whole post-modern impulse in art is a fundamental mistake, more a symptom of the ills of the times than a remedy for them. But I wonder if this standpoint does not run the risk of becoming a reactionary one, unable to adequately comprehend the development of contemporary art in its own terms. This would be all the more remarkable inasmuch as the whole thrust of Arnheim's career has been to defend modernism against its conservative detractors. In fact, the very standard that led him to champion modernism, namely the primacy of expressive form as embodied in the structure of the work, is what caused him to reject the post-modernist impulse toward de-structuring.

The congruence of Gestalt psychology and modernist art rests, I believe, on the notion of the expressive totality. In either the percept or the work of art, meaning is contained in the structure, which gives coherence to the parts of a whole. Without the dynamic structural unity of the whole, meaning cannot be expressed. As Arnheim has emphasized, this structure need not be simple or regular. Because meaning is often complex, the work of art must admit tension and complexity as intrinsic to its structural wholeness. Nevertheless, in his view, this complexity cannot lead to disorder or else the work will lose the capacity for expression that is its reason for being. For Arnheim, an ambiguous, confused or contradictory work is a failure. Even the expression of disorder requires order. A work may seek to express the chaos of our times, but it must contain this chaos within an orderly structure or lose its capacity to express meaning altogether.

Arnheim does recognize that there are different ways of arriving at order. In *The Dynamics of Architectural Form*, he distinguishes between order imposed 'from above' and order emerging 'from below.' It makes a difference whether order comes from an overarching framework that integrates the component parts of a structure or whether it emerges from the interplay of these parts as a by-product of their mutual relationship. Although Arnheim clearly has a preference for the former, seeing order 'from below' as the expression of an atomized society that lacks an integrative principle of being, nevertheless he recognizes the legitimacy of the order that emerges 'from below' as a possible way of attaining wholeness. He compares it to 'the attempt of a group of musicians to improvise a piece of music…Together the musicians search for the theme of the whole. It is a spirit of collective cooperation, not of atomistic competition' (Arnheim 1977, p.196).

This distinction between two ways of attaining order is a suggestive one and comes close to accounting for some tendencies in contemporary life and art; however, it still assumes the primacy of order *tout court*. Whether from above or below, according to Arnheim, the result must be a structured totality expressive of meaning in order for it to be art. This is perhaps the very point of contestation in post-modernist art and thought. Is it still possible to embrace the notion of wholeness as a fundamental principle? The encounter with Arnheim's psychology of art demands that we raise this question.

It seems to me that one of the dominant features of our age is an overwhelming sense of chaos and fragmentation. Not only have larger social units like the nation-state broken down, but also the micro-units of family and community no longer provide a coherent basis for social life and individual development. In fact, even the notion of the individual as a coherent totality has become suspect. Given the fragmented character of our lives, is the Enlightenment concept of the autonomous individual still relevant? The psychologist Robert J. Lifton (1993) suggests that the best we can do is to celebrate the fluid and 'Protean' character of the self, capable of changing in changing circumstances.

If the critique of totality were based solely on the break-down of social relations, then Arnheim's standpoint would still be the appropriate one: to uphold the standard of order in the face of an emerging chaos. However, the challenge of post-modernism, as I understand it, is that it sees the very notion of totality as an illusion, an ideological banner that masks the intrinsic chaos of existence. Thus the totalitarian state or the religious cult are logical outcomes of the liberal allegiance to wholeness, not departures from it.

This attack on the notion of totality can be traced at least as far back as Kant, who saw the concept of the whole as a dialectical illusion. As we are ourselves part of the totality we claim to know, our knowledge of it can only be partial and relative to our perspective. We are not capable of a god-like survey of the universe. As embodied beings, subject to the conditions of space and time, our knowledge goes only as far as the limits of our possible experience. For Kant, any claim to a totalizing knowledge is relegated to the field of dogmatic metaphysics.

Heidegger and Derrida have elaborated Kant's critique of metaphysics to show that the entire history of Western philosophy rests on what Derrida calls the 'metaphysics of presence,' the belief that truth can be bodily present in the moment. The metaphysics of presence rejects time and historicity in favor of a spatial conception of objectivity in which the world is seen as present-to-hand. The model for this knowledge is the sense of sight.

Vision, in this analysis, presents objects in their simultaneous co-presence. The philosophical tradition, based on the metaphysics of presence, values vision as the sense that comes closest to true knowledge, since sight provides the immediate presence that is a sign of truth. Thus, the primary metaphors for knowledge in the West derive from sight: if, as Arnheim put it, eyesight is insight, then the converse is also true: insight is eyesight. Knowing, in this tradition, is understood as a form of seeing.

If it is true that seeing, understood in this way, misleads by presenting a world that is present-at-hand, are there other senses that might serve us better? Several thinkers have noticed the difference between Greek philosophy with its emphasis on sight (the philosopher 'sees' the truth; the truth is what is visible to the intellect) and the Hebrew Bible's emphasis on hearing (God 'speaks' to the Israelites; the primary refrain for the communication of truth to God's people is, 'Hear, O Israel!'). Hearing, of course, is a sense primarily dependent upon time rather than space. It attends to 'what is' as a temporally contextualized message rather than as a spatially displayed object.

The emphasis on audition in contemporary thought goes with a recognition of the role of language in the formation of human being. From this perspective, we are essentially speaking beings, and our speech is a conversation that binds us in a discourse that never ends. There is always more to be said, and we will never say it all, never express the totality of our being in one present moment. The wish to do so leads us astray.

Is Arnheim's work subject to the critique of the metaphysics of presence? Is it, in spite of its modernist sympathies, beholden to a traditional philosophy of totality? Certainly Arnheim emphasizes the concept of structure. Although he gives a subtle analysis of the relationship between order and disorder, he does not make the concept of order into a problem. For Arnheim, order is the touchstone for aesthetic and cultural criticism.

Similarly, Arnheim takes his stand on the primacy of the visible. Vision is understood to be the royal road to truth. The objectivity, detachment and universality belonging to the visual field are taken as the essential characteristics of knowledge. Arnheim is sensitive to the effects of context upon visible form, but he does not seem to include himself as a theorist within the context. He often refers to himself as an observer and strives to maintain the position of detached objectivity that observation affords.

Furthermore, Arnheim consistently gives precedence to spatial relations over temporal ones. Even music is understood by him in a spatial sense: the melody needs to be surveyed as a whole in order to be understood. Thus, it seems to me that temporal process tends to give way to spatial structure in Arnheim's understanding of art.

Finally, language is given a secondary place in Arnheim's thinking in terms of its access to the real. Because language is discursive, it can never achieve the simultaneous co-presence of the parts that a true totality demands. In fact, Arnheim (1969) seeks to show that all valid thinking is essentially visual thinking: the sensible image contains the truth expressed through words. For him, language approaches truth only in so far as it embodies the visual.

Arnheim's perspective has important implications for the theory and practice of the arts therapies. In the first place, it is clear that art, for Arnheim, is oriented toward the world and not the self. At several points in his writings, he inveighs against 'self-expression.' The goal of artists is not to express themselves, but rather to find the form for a more universal truth that can be shared by all.

Similarly, the purpose of artistic creativity is not to express one's emotions, but to give form to one's thoughts. Art is primarily a cognitive, not an emotional, activity. In *New Essays on the Psychology of Art* (1986), Arnheim states, 'My own bias is that the arts fulfill, first of all, a cognitive function' (1986, p.253). A journal entry of 1978 characteristically notes that,

> Far from 'expressing his emotions,' a good composer confines his feelings to his private life. When I hear music outpouring joy or suffering, I turn off the radio, irritated by someone inconsiderate enough to importune me with his own business. (Arnheim 1986, p.234)

In fact, Arnheim has a rather negative view of the very concept of emotion. In his article, 'Emotion and Feeling in Psychology and Art,' Arnheim (1966) suggests that emotion is a 'label that stops research.' Far from being a specific state of mind, emotion refers only to the *tension or excitement level*, produced by the interaction of mental forces... Thus, emotion does not contribute impulses of its own; it is merely the effect of the play of forces taking place within the mind' (Arnheim 1966, p.310, italics in original).

Arnheim is not denying the role of emotion in mental life or in the arts. However, he is trying to show that what counts in art is the dynamic structure of the percept. What we call 'emotion' refers primarily, in his view, to the degree of tension produced by our perception of a significant whole. Although art has an emotional resonance, this is a by-product and not the source of artistic creativity.

One would expect Arnheim, then, to be rather unsympathetic to art therapy, in which the expression of the self and, particularly, the emotional component of the self, has been considered to be primary. In fact, however, Arnheim sees himself as a friend of art therapy, viewing it as a legitimate method for healing the disorderly world of the patient.

Again, it is in terms of the primacy of order that Arnheim approaches the topic. The art therapist, for him, helps patients to find a structural form in art that is missing in their own turbulent inner world. Thus, art becomes 'the creation of a meaningful order offering a refuge from the unmanageable confusion of the outer reality.' In fact, Arnheim suggests, the alienation of many contemporary artists could be overcome if they took a lesson from art therapists: 'the blessings experienced in therapy… can remind artists everywhere what the function of art has always been and will always be' (Arnheim 1992, p.170).

Although Arnheim did not develop a theory of art therapy, I believe that one could clearly derive such a theory from his work. First, the primacy of sensible experience in Arnheim's writings indicates that 'talk therapy' would be an incomplete form of treatment addressing only a partial component of the personality. The human personality is expressed through bodily presence in the world. Any breakdown of this personality requires a treatment that is an adequate response to this bodily presence. Therapy must, therefore, be a therapy of the senses in order to be a therapy of the soul.

Second, Arnheim's analysis of the arts shows that art is a primary way of expressing our being-in-the-world. Art uses the media of the senses as its forms of expression. In so doing, art raises the capacity of our senses to a reflective and conscious level. The therapy of the senses must then be a therapy through art.

Moreover, I believe it is a fair conclusion to be drawn from Arnheim's writings to see art therapy as a primary rather than adjunctive mode of treatment. Art therapy is not a supplement to the 'real' treatment carried out in verbal psychotherapy. Rather, by addressing the core of the personality, art therapy places itself at the center of therapeutic work.

This justification of art therapy, however, also implies a certain view of its nature. Within Arnheim's framework, mental illness would have to be seen as a breakdown of structure. In Yeats' words (2000, p.158), quoted often throughout this book, 'Things fall apart; the centre cannot hold.' The integrated nature of the human personality, in which all the parts form a harmonious though complex whole, would be destroyed. Whether through schizoid withdrawal into simplicity or catabolic breakdown into a chaos of conflicting parts, the overall unity of the personality would be lost.

Consequently, the goal of art therapy would be to restore the structural wholeness of the personality. The arts, as the highest embodiments of order, structure and balance, would serve to re-integrate the discordant elements of the person and to enable him or her to express the complex meaning of their life in a significant form. The therapeutic value of the arts, for Arnheim, consists in their capacity to bring order to a dis-ordered soul. Art therapy can overcome inner chaos by providing the means to structural integration.

I have attempted here to draw some conclusions, in accordance with the general tendencies of Arnheim's thinking, as to what a theory of art therapy based upon his principles might look like. Among contemporary art therapists, Shaun McNiff (1981), in particular, has been influenced by Arnheim's work and has attempted to integrate his emphasis on structure with an appreciation of the possibilities of spontaneous play.

In general, it seems to me that Arnheim's thinking does provide the basis for a coherent framework for the practice of art therapy. Grounded in a scientific psychology and the humanistic practice of the history of art, Arnheim's theory of artistic expression offers a conception of human nature that explains the necessity and effectiveness of the therapeutic use of the arts. Such a conception seems to me to be necessary if art therapy is to achieve an understanding of its own possibility. Moreover, the emphasis on structure in Arnheim's psychology goes a long way to explaining both mental illness and the kind of treatment that it requires. If illness is the result of a breakdown of structure, then the cure would seem to be a re-structuring and re-integration of the personality. Art therapy would be important as a means of carrying out such a re-integration.

However, I wonder whether the consistent emphasis on structure and the consequent opposition to chaos and break-down in Arnheim's work can also be seen as possible limitations. Just as post-modernism in philosophy and the arts has challenged Arnheim's conception of art and its role in the modern world, so a similar trend in psychological thought can be understood to be a challenge to any conception of art therapy that can be drawn from Arnheim's writings.

It is questionable whether the personality, any more than the world, can be properly understood as a structured totality. In Jacques Lacan's view (1977a) of the development of the subject, for example, the integral self, capable of grasping its wholeness in a glance, is the product of an imaginary identification in the mirror stage of development. The child, according to Lacan (1977a), experiences its own fragmentation, but wishes to escape from the chaos that this implies. Accordingly, when it grasps its image in the mirror (or in the gaze of the one who mirrors it), the child eagerly seizes upon this image as an expression of its true identity. The adult, consequently, who remains in this imaginary stage of identification, will search always for the person, institution, work of art or, for that matter, theory, that reinforces his or her view of themselves as an integrated whole (Lacan 1977b). As Lacan once remarked, 'The idea of the unifying unity of the human condition has always had on me the effect of a scandalous lie' (Lacan 1972, p.190).

Lacan's solution, ultimately, is to transcend the imaginary in the direction of the symbolic, which demands the recognition of otherness as an essential component of the self. As Rimbaud (1975, p.128) said, *'Je est un autre.'* I am different from myself, and I can only express this difference in modes of signifying that point beyond themselves. This perspective accounts for Lacan's preference for surrealist poetry as well as his own well-known gnomic style.

One need not be a Lacanian to take seriously his questioning of the principle of totality as it applies to the personality. Is the integrated self a myth that we invent to avoid our fragmentation? Is chaos more than a mere reflection of a disordered period of history? Does it perhaps express an essential truth about the human condition? If so, then how can we distinguish the chaotic effects of catabolic breakdown from the 'normal' non-identity of the subject?

Furthermore, if chaos is intrinsic to human being, is it appropriate to treat catabolic breakdown by means of the building up of order? Might it not be more appropriate to find creative forms of disorder to match the energy of a fragmented self? I believe D.W. Winnicott's concept of 'formlessness' comes close to this kind of perspective. It could be interesting to contrast a conception of art therapy based on the notion of formlessness with Arnheim's emphasis on structure.

For Winnicott (2005 [1971]), the analyst's attempt to find order in the patient's chaotic presentation of self often reflects anxiety on the analyst's own part. The latter fears his or her own internal fragmentation and thus strives for wholeness by foreclosing the space of formlessness that the analytic encounter produces. As a result, the patient either remains stuck in an adaptive mode of behavior, the 'false self' system, or else internalizes the aggression produced by a thwarted creative expression of self and enters into depression.

If the analyst were able, instead, to tolerate a period of formlessness, then a creative use of symbol formation might emerge. Winnicott described this dwelling in formlessness as a rudimentary form of play. The notion of formlessness as play needs to be correlated with Winnicott's well-known conception of transitional space. The transitional space between self and other is a space without the clarity of oppositions that enables order to be achieved. Transitional space is disorderly, multiple, ambiguous and confused. Meaning has not yet emerged. For this reason, it is impossible to know or control what takes place within this space. Being-with replaces doing, as purposive activity gives way to just letting-be.

If we recall that the notion of transitional space is seen by Winnicott as the model for all creative experience as well as for the practice of art, then the consequences for art therapy become clear. From this perspective, art therapy cannot be understood as an attempt to find or produce order within the disorderly inner world of the client. Rather, play and art are used as forms of formlessness – as media for attaining the state of productive unintegration that allows for the creative attainment of meaning.

If we were to develop a theory of art therapy based on a chaotic or unintegrated view of the self, would it not emphasize spontaneity, play and improvisation rather than structure, form and balance? Would it not be more accepting of aggression in its capacity to de-structure an imaginary order? Would it, therefore, not encourage formlessness as an essential way of being rather than always seek to find orderly outcomes?

On the other hand, Arnheim reminds us that formlessness is not enough. The work of art always presents itself as an ordered whole. Can we demand any less for the products of art therapy? To see a patient's work as only self-expression would be to limit it just as much as if we were to see it as only a formal structure. Form and feeling go together. As McNiff (1981, p.39) states, 'art intensifies feeling while simultaneously providing a protective and guiding structure.'

Ultimately, perhaps, it is not a question of an 'either-or' – either structure or chaos, either form or formlessness. Perhaps each has its place within a fully developed theory of art therapy. Arnheim takes us as far as we can go in one direction. A balanced view might wish to incorporate the counter-perspective to his own.

Arnheim's emphasis upon structure results from taking the point of view of the observer. As he has himself noted, 'my life has been one of contemplation rather than action; and since I watch the artists, who are contemplators, I am twice-removed from active life... I am...the little owl perched on the shoulder of Athene' (1989, p.369). The little owl, of course, represents wisdom, the wisdom that comes from witnessing the tumult of history.

Rudolph Arnheim was a witness to the chaos of the past century as well as to the creative attempts of artists to overcome it. His work is a testament to the human capacity to master disorder and to find meaning and balance in the world through artistic creativity. His writings testify to the nobility of art. In the new millennium, however, we can only wonder whether this nobility is enough, whether it can contain the tendencies to destruction that we see around us.

Can the arts resist the catabolic breakdown of our culture, or is it necessary to find new forms to express and live with this catabolism? Perhaps, in a homeopathic manner, these forms will themselves embody some of the chaos that they encounter. In that case, we might well ask with Yeats (2000, p.158):

> what rough beast, its hour come round at last,
> Slouches towards Bethlehem to be born?

6

# Is Order Enough?
# Is Chaos too Much?

## *Art, Therapy and the Search for Wholeness*
## *— A Dialogue with Ellen Levine*

*Ellen Levine*: I'd like to talk about the connection between order and disorder, how that connection is involved in the process of making art as well as in the relationship of the artist to the work of art.

*Stephen K. Levine*: Is it involved in the relationship of the viewer to the work as well?

*EL*: I'm not as interested in the viewer in this regard. What I have noticed in my own painting is how naturally order comes to be there for me when I don't even try. When I try to have things be disordered, they keep finding a sense of order.

*SL*: What actually takes place? Could you be specific about the way that happens in terms of your use of form? I know your paintings are somewhat abstract; you have called them 'abstract landscapes.' They don't have clear representational images of particular places, and yet they are certainly reminiscent of places that have been important for you, like the shoreline of Martha's Vineyard where you have spent so much time. Now, is it your intention when you start a painting to find a form that would somehow represent this landscape, or does it just happen to come out that way?

*EL*: Sometimes I do a series of works where I begin with something, then I find a part of it that I like and that I want to elaborate on in another painting. So, in this case, I am expanding upon something that has already been formed. But the original starting point is usually without any sense of what it is that I want to make. It seems like there is never any plan to it.

Sometimes it has to do with finding new materials at the art store that I want to experiment with, or the music that I'm listening to that moves me in a certain way. But even though I always start from a fresh place, there's a theme that keeps emerging, a kind of ordering that comes about, so that my style now seems to be easily recognizable to people. It's not something that I plan beforehand. It seems that I have an innate sense of order or an innate thematic that keeps playing itself out.

*SL*: I wonder if this isn't a different way of thinking about art-making than in traditional aesthetics. In my understanding of that tradition, the artist is conceived of as having an idea of form in his or her mind before creating the work. Aristotle, for example, thought that the form is used as a guiding principle to shape the material, so that the end result is the embodiment of the form. But what I hear you saying is very close to what I was trying to get at in the chapter on Arnheim: the form is never there to begin with. The form is always what emerges from a somewhat chaotic process of making.

*EL*: Actually, when I hear you talking now it's still a little different from what I do. I feel that the forms are already embodied in nature. The form that keeps coming up is a form that I know from the natural landscape I perceive. But, of course, it's translated by me into an essential shape. The relationships of lines and spaces remain the same, but the way that I interpret them changes. Sometimes I jumble things up or use very odd colors that one would not associate with this particular landscape. If you were to actually perceive the real place, it would be a surprise to find certain colors in the landscape that I have painted. It's a kind of spin that I put on it, and yet there is something that really corresponds to the natural forms and the imaginal forms. So it's a little bit different from a traditional aesthetic, and different as well from something that works totally out of chaos. I think that I do have an order, but it's the order that is in the forms themselves as perceived.

*SL*: That phrase 'as perceived' is very important. Arnheim would certainly agree. It's your perception of nature that is the key to your transformation of forms in art.

*EL*: If I have an intention to paint something in nature, my judgment and my rational functions come up, and I am quite blocked or paralyzed in doing that. I am usually not satisfied at all with copying reality. I like the accidental quality of what emerges as I play in-between my perceptions and my imagination. The forms are caught for a moment between two worlds.

*SL*: I like that quality of being in-between. Often a viewer will have a sense of being caught up in an art-work, having a relationship with it, so that it's not clear where the meaning resides – in the work or in the person perceiving it. We can't distance ourselves and look at the work as an object of our experience.

*EL*: Yes, I think when I am painting, that is precisely what I am experiencing. I'm not copying a picture, and I'm not going out into the landscape and doing a work that is representational. But I am usually in a place with no windows and with artificial light; I am going into my imagination there. The images are coming up and I am responding to them. I ask, 'What do you need next?' And I follow the trails that the paint makes, or I use my hands. What does the image ask of me to do next? It often seems to me to ask for balance, order and composition. But I have to force myself to be more playful with it, to experiment more with different ways of working with it – sometimes to destroy it or to blot it out and then try something new. It is always an interaction between the image and myself. We're in a dance together, or in a dialogue.

I'm not an objective painter who tries to take a distance from the work. Maybe after the painting is completed, I could find a distance from it, look at it and talk about it. But there is no such distance when I am working.

*SL*: In your most recent work, such as the cover of this book, you seem to have moved from being inspired by the landscape to starting from images of war and devastation taken from the newspapers. How would you account for that change?

*EL*: I think that I am working on two levels lately. I am still fascinated with the ocean/sky configuration in the landscape and especially where they meet in the horizon line. But something mysterious and ominous has crept into these forms. I feel the weight of the world entering these more serene forms and disturbing them, creating a feeling of unease. This is also the feeling I get these days about what is happening in the world. When I look at the newspapers and see some of the photographs from Iraq or the Middle East, they look like paintings. Some of the photojournalism is crafted so well, it stirs me and I cannot take my eyes off the image. I put these images into my paintings as a way of calling attention to them. When we read the newspaper, it is often with a sense of detachment or even numbness. By taking the image out of the newspaper and highlighting it, I am almost forcing myself – and the viewer – to encounter it. Some of my paintings are beginning to contain both the disturbing images in the sea or sky and the photographs from the newspapers. This is the newest development in my work.

*SL*: To me, it's as if you are trying to come to terms with the chaos in the world and to find some place for it in the order of the landscape. Was that your intention?

*EL*: I really hadn't thought of it in these terms, but it does make sense to me. Many of my photographic images are faces of children who are in dangerous situations. Their reactions are showing in their expressions. I put them in landscapes which are stormy and unsettled but that might offer them a sense of protection. However, this protection is rather fragile – a roof made of sticks that looks like it could blow away, for example. How could I ever stop this violence or think that I could protect the children from it? I can only imagine myself doing this in the form of the painting. The hope comes from showing it by means of the order of the painting.

*SL*: Let's shift the discussion to your work as an art therapist. In working with patients, whether children or adults, how can we understand the relevance of these ideas concerning chaos and order? What do you think takes place in the client's art-making?

*EL*: What I actually start thinking about is the making of the relationship itself, which is the first work and, in a sense, the first form of order that you make together. You build a relationship together, a container if you will, so that the disturbance can be held. And there are various ways of going about that. For me, working with someone, a child or an adult, has a lot to do with experiencing, perhaps in a formless way at first, where this person is going to take the relationship, what he or she is needing, and how the relationship is going to be shaped by the person and by myself. And that takes place in a process of not-knowing. As much as you want to know, you ultimately cannot know what direction you are going to go in. It's the same in working with the arts as it is with people. It's a participation in not-knowing. This is really important. Giving up to an exploration is crucial. However, ultimately it leads to some kind of order. Someone working within Arnheim's perspective would find meaning in the order that comes from working with a person. Health comes from finding the form of a person's work or life.

*SL*: Arnheim doesn't talk about the therapeutic process itself, aside from a few incidental remarks. Within his framework, though, therapy would focus on the integration of different structures so that ultimately the person would be able to contain, within the totality of his or her life, the richness of all the diverse areas of experience. That would be, in his terms, an 'anabolic' tendency toward complexity. In working with a client, the goal, for Arnheim, would have to be the integration of all the split-off parts of the psyche that were in conflict and that were, therefore, producing pain and suffering.

*EL*: Would it be to bring together and to integrate all these split-off parts into a theme that would be manifested in the work of art in the therapeutic context?

*SL*: Yes, the theme might be capable of expressing the complexity of conflicting structures. Using your own work again as an example, one could say that the theme that you work over and over again integrates your memories of the landscape of Martha's Vineyard with the imaginal longing for that place when you are not there. The landscape then becomes the container for the chaos and disorder of the world. Arnheim might argue that here is a good example of the very principle of integration that he recommends, even though it sounds as if you are coming out of chaos.

I think that it is easy to get polarized in this discussion between ideas of order and disorder. One way to avoid this is to focus on the different moments of the artistic process. Are we focusing on the end result, which may involve a high order of integration, or are we focusing on the process itself, which involves, for most artists, at least a certain period of not knowing and not being able to control what is going on?

*EL*: And also not being able to create, being blocked with no images coming, a lot of frustration and disappointment.

*SL*: Yes, the emptiness of the void seems to be part of the creative process as well. I want to get back to the question of post-modernism at this point. This question interests me as a challenge to any integrative theory of art. Post-modernism seems to be saying that the whole idea of integration is an illusion, actually a pernicious one that ends up with splitting off certain parts of our experience that can't be integrated. It's always a kind of foreclosed totality. No structure is big enough to include all the parts of our experience; and the ones that seem to be capable of this do so at the expense of splitting, and consequently of projecting the rejected parts.

*EL*: What about this thing that I struggle with within myself: my natural tendency to produce order? This could be a characterological tendency. And I wonder about so many art therapists now who talk about integration and wholeness and pulling together all the split-off parts, as well as the emphasis in our field on healing, with the sense that something can be healed once and for all. This seems like a fantasy of Eden, a time when there were no splits and no conflicts. It reminds me of people who think that peace means the end of all conflict, who have a notion of total harmony. What do we do about this impulse toward conflict-free harmony? Is this the myth of our era? At the same time, we do need to make sense out of our experience and find meaning in it. Are you saying that there is no meaning in our experience?

*SL*: No, I don't think I am saying that. What I am saying is that there may be multiple meanings, that no one meaning, no matter how complex, is capable of grasping the variety of life. I like the idea of characterological differences between different theorists. I certainly recognize in myself more of a tendency toward multiplicity than toward unity or unification. I'm much more interested in processes that break down and fall apart and seem to be chaotic but end up perhaps with meaning, at least with a great deal of variety and richness. That's one of the reasons why in my own art-making, besides poetry, I work mostly in improvisatory theatre and in clown. In improvisation, there is always a feeling of being at risk, of not knowing and not being able to control what is going on, but also of having the faith that if you allow a creative process to take place, something will emerge that will have value. I like very much the work of the clown who always introduces disorder and chaos into every seemingly orderly situation. Now, whether this is purely characterological or not is debatable.

*EL*: What I have enjoyed in my own work with clowning is to take my tendency toward order and to play with it, to bring this tendency out in its most exaggerated form, one that is completely absurd. My clown work is about being able to control the world, whereas I actually think that on some level things are totally out of control and that it's not possible to control our environment. We can control small aspects of our lives, but in general the world is not subject to our control.

*SL*: That's right, and I think there is a question of whether it can be. But I would like to go back to your statement about the emphasis on healing and wholeness. I think you are right in putting them together; 'healing' etymologically relates to becoming 'whole.' The important thing is to distinguish between Arnheim's position and a tendency that I see in the expressive therapies that I think is particularly problematic. This tendency would be to look for a totality that is harmonious and without tension. The overcoming of tension is thus somehow conceived of as wholeness.

Arnheim is clear that this would be a simplistic solution. Human existence is so complex that the only kind of art-works that could do justice to it are works that include a tremendous capacity for tension. In fact, Arnheim sees the tendency toward tension as one of the sources of pleasure in art. So for him the concept of a perceptual whole is not harmonious in the sense of a percept without any tension. The wholeness is a wholeness of directed tension, in which the dynamic forces in one part of the field are balanced by the forces in another. In any work of art there is a great deal of aliveness and vitality. The forms are alive; they're moving; they're tending toward a certain outcome. These forms are counterbalanced by others tending toward different outcomes.

*EL*: What you're saying is interesting if you don't think about a work of art, but about an individual's life or about a family system. In these cases, the idea of a balance of tension would be a more creative resolution as an outcome of therapy than the idea of wholeness that I am describing.

*SL*: Yes. I particularly find objectionable the use of the arts to achieve this kind of tensionless wholeness. Then you usually get quite insipid art.

*EL*: Static, uninteresting works.

*SL*: I don't think that Arnheim is at all recommending the same thing as the conflict-free concept of wholeness, but he does emphasize the importance of an integrative whole. Because Arnheim makes the best possible case for integration, it's worthwhile to encounter his thinking from a post-modern perspective, and ask whether it's adequate for understanding our situation.

*EL*: But doesn't post-modernism err on the other side, of being so much a philosophy of fragmentation and the celebration of fragmentation, that there is nothing that holds the center together because there is no center? Where does that leave us in terms of our experience of ourselves and the world?

*SL*: It leaves us with a question: whether we can live in a decentered world or with a decentered sense of self, whether multiplicity or what James Hillman has called 'polytheism' is enough (Hillman 1975). Do we need a center, do we need a guiding principle? In that case, where is it, where can we find it? I think the notion that if we can't find a central meaning in our life, then we can find it in art, is hard to take. In that case, we're saying that art is really illusion, that art promises a unification and a totalization that is impossible in the real world. In a way, art then becomes less meaningful.

The most interesting artists today, like the writer Roberto Bolaño, have moved away from the notion of a central meaning that structures the entire work. In literature, for example, narrative authority is more and more rejected by writers. Who knows what's going on in these works? Who can say what it all means? Who is the main character? Is there a hero or protagonist who goes through a course of development in post-modern fiction, as she would in classic novels? I don't think so. In the writing of Pynchon or Bolaño, for example, identity is always shifting; it's unclear who the central character is, let alone what the plot is, what the author's position is, and how the reader is implicated in the text. Now, some people don't like this style of writing, purely as a matter of taste. It can be quite unsettling.

*EL*: But somehow these works have become touchstones for our epoch because people often do experience their lives in this way.

*SL*: That's right. Other kinds of work can seem boring. We want an art that corresponds to our experience of chaos, at least I do. Other forms of art run the risk of being irrelevant, even though, to a great extent, these are in fact the forms of mass entertainment.

*EL*: People want to see things that have a beginning, a middle and an end.

*SL*: Yes, we want desperately to cling to the notion of a coherent world and self.

*EL*: I think for us the danger in the field of expressive arts therapy is to begin to cling like that. If we do, we'll lose the connection to what is really happening in our lives; our work will become an ideology rather than a practice.

*SL*: I agree with you. What happens is that people go into therapy to find a wholeness that is lacking in their lives. They may indeed find this wholeness in therapy, but it will have to remain in therapy because there is no place for it in the world in which they live. People then become addicted to therapy and want to keep going back to the experience of wholeness that they had at that moment in that setting. What I wonder is, can we use our work as artists and as therapists to help our clients to live with multiplicity? To enable them to tolerate ambiguity, paradox and loss of control, and even to be able to play with the chaos that they find in the world? Then I think therapy would have a useful purpose.

*EL*: Perhaps the way we can tolerate and even embrace ambiguity and multiplicity is by forming therapeutic relationships in which the imagination can be given free play. Within the order of the relationship, there can be room for the chaos of art. Arnheim would accept the idea of striving for a relationship complex enough to encompass chaos. Human beings can tolerate a high degree of disorder, but only within a framework that can contain it and allow for the emergence of new forms. The therapeutic relationship holds the promise of allowing new forms of both art- and soul-making to emerge.

# 7

# The Expressive Body

## *A Fragmented Totality*

Expressive arts therapy is distinguished from other modes of therapeutic practice by its emphasis on bodily expression. It is the body that dances, sings, makes music, paints, sculpts, enacts scenes and speaks poetically. How is it that bodily expression can be therapeutic? Is there what we could call a 'healing' function to the expressive body? As we have said, to heal, in its etymological sense, is to make whole. In order to understand whether bodily expression can heal, we must first look at the ways in which we are said to suffer from a lack of wholeness. Is wholeness the normal state of a healthy organism or is it an illusion that keeps us from living with our deficiencies? Can there be a form of wholeness that encompasses chaos and fragmentation? How might we understand this conception of wholeness in relationship to our bodily experience?

I would like to explore these questions here by presenting two contrasting views on bodily expression, those of Jacques Lacan and Maurice Merleau-Ponty. Lacan, a psychoanalyst, and Merleau-Ponty, a philosopher, were French theorists who have been immensely influential in shaping contemporary European psychoanalytic and philosophical thought. However, although each of them influenced the other, they held diametrically opposed views on the role of the body in cultural life. A consideration of the differences between their positions will, I believe, help provide a framework within which a better understanding of the possible healing function of bodily expression can be developed.

I will begin with a presentation of Lacan's views on the fragmentary nature of bodily experience. An exploration of his perspective will show us the limitations of a therapeutic approach based on a relational, holistic model that does not take account of this fragmentation. At the same time, I will argue that Lacan's own one-sidedness and his lack of a positive conception of the body prevents us from seeing the value of a bodily oriented expressive therapy. Consequently, I will turn to Merleau-Ponty for a phenomenological analysis of bodily experience that can be used to account for the body's role in healing, an analysis that takes into account the 'ambiguity' and chaotic character of this experience. Finally, I will outline a conception of expressive arts therapy that recognizes its own limitations, but that nevertheless offers grounds for hope that human suffering can be expressed and witnessed in an aesthetically responsible way (Knill *et al.* 2005).

This chapter, then, uses the hermeneutic approach of interpreting a tradition of inquiry in order to develop a position adequate for our own situation. To answer our question about the possible healing function of the expressive body, we need to look at alternative conceptions of bodily experience and engage in a dialogue with these different perspectives. Out of this dialogue, we hope that a new image of expressive arts therapy will begin to emerge, one that takes account both of the fragmentary nature of bodily experience and of the human drive towards healing and wholeness.

We begin with a text by Jacques Lacan, 'The Mirror Stage as Formative of the Function of the I as Revealed in Psychoanalytic Experience' (1977a). In this text, first delivered as an address to the Sixteenth International Congress of Psychoanalysis held in Zurich in 1949, Lacan developed a critique of ego psychology based on the early experience of the child's recognition of its image in a mirror. The child sees the image of its body and has an 'Aha-experience': 'That is me!' This experience gives it the beginnings of a sense of identity. From the point of view of the psychology of the ego, this early identification of the child with its image in the mirror (or in mirroring experiences with others) is the basis of a stable sense of self.

Lacan would agree with this assessment of the role of the mirror stage, except that for him the question arises of the difference between the image of the self reflected in the mirror and the actual experience of the child's own body. The image is of a unitary being; I see myself as whole and in command of the parts of my body. For that reason, I like to stand in front of the mirror and manipulate my body so that the image changes according to my will. It seems that the image obeys me. In fact, thought Lacan, it is I who am captivated by the image. I become a slave to this identificatory image of wholeness and desire to become it, to assume it in my being. This is, in fact, impossible, for the child's experience is actually one of bodily fragmentation.

Due to what Lacan called the 'specific prematurity of birth in man' (Lacan 1977a, p.96), the child's experience of its body is one of uncoordination, of something that cannot be controlled or surveyed as a whole. This fragmented body (*corps morcelé*) is very different from the unitary, cohesive entity that I behold in the mirror. The image promises relief from this lack of being that I am; therefore I seek to become it. Later, when I encounter others in a social world, I will try to have them confirm my imaginary identification of myself; I will want them to see me as I want to see myself. This narcissistic desire brings aggressivity into human relationships.

The 'I' that emerges out of the mirror phase is, for Lacan, based on an experience of alienation. Any psychology of the ego that takes this alienating experience as the foundation for a concept of the self is doomed to be based on misunderstanding (*méconnaissance*). Therapist and patient will play a mirror game with each other in which each tries to be seen as a whole person in order to avoid the suffering that lies at the heart of the fragmented experience of bodily existence. Psychoanalytic experience is testimony to the ruses in which the subject will engage in order to maintain his identity.

For Lacan, the only way out of this impasse is to introduce a third term between two subjects struggling for a mistaken recognition: language. It is only in language that I am able to enter into a dialogue with another, a dialogue in which we both accept that truth cannot be captured on the level of the imaginary. Language, unlike visual imagery, is based on a system of differences that forever prevents the subject from freezing herself into a static identity. By entering into the field of language contained in the psychoanalytic dialogue (in which the body is put out of play), I implicitly renounce my narcissistic desire for wholeness, for an identity based on knowledge and control.

Lacan sees the symbolic dimension of language as having the capacity to overcome the limitations inherent in the bodily imaginary. The task of psychoanalytic discourse then becomes the breaking of the imaginary identifications in which I imprison myself. In that sense, psychoanalysis is iconoclastic; rather than aiming at the formation of ego identity, it aims at the destruction of the idols of the self. Only on that basis can the plenitude of signification be released.

Lacanian thought poses certain challenges to the theoretical foundations of expressive arts therapy. First, Lacan illuminates the narcissism contained in the act of expression. In a sense, all art has a performative aspect; it demands to be seen by another. Is there not, in this desire to be seen, a trace of the 'Look at me!' that animates the child's relation with its parents? The emptiness that actors experience after a show is based on more than physical exhaustion; it also stems from the realization that the image they present to others can never be identical with their own existence.

From a Lacanian perspective, therefore, it is a misunderstanding to think that art can heal suffering. The imaginary identifications that the aesthetic realm offers are seductions that divert us from the fragmented character of our embodied experience. Only an art dedicated to overcoming the ego could compete with the deconstruction offered by the psychoanalytic experience. Lacan himself located such an art in surrealist poetry, based on the automatic writing experiments that themselves derive from the free association of analytic speech. In this poetic style, one can only say that 'it' speaks; language itself is the author of the poem. The 'I' completely disappears in the flow of words. In general, however, for Lacan, art is always subject to the temptation of captivation by the imaginary.

Second, Lacan's thinking puts into question the notion of the therapeutic relationship implicitly maintained by many expressive arts therapists. Relational models of psychotherapy stemming from both object relations theory and self-psychology (often framed within a feminist perspective) seem to imply that the healing effect of expressive arts therapy comes from the recognition of the self by the other. Patients or clients express themselves in the work; the therapist recognizes and accepts this expression of self and thereby helps to heal the wounds to the self that occurred in the child's early experience of being with others.

From the point of view of Lacanian analysis, misunderstanding is at its height in this relational model. The mother–infant dyad on which the model is based takes place within the imaginary realm of identification. Certainly the infant wants to be seen by mother, but this seeing only fosters the illusion of wholeness by which the child seeks to escape its fragmentary being. If therapy tries to re-create a relationship based on the imaginary, it will avoid the difficult task of deconstructing the ego, which alone can lead to psychic freedom.

Thus Lacan's critique of the imaginary challenges not only our conception of the role of the arts in psychotherapy but also the nature of the therapeutic relationship itself. We must therefore ask, what kind of healing, if any, can be contained in the expressive act? And in what way do I need to be with another so as to make this healing possible? Most significantly, for our purposes, we need to inquire how the body can be the medium of expressive arts therapy when the suffering contained in bodily fragmentation is the motivating factor behind my escape from myself.

For it is not only the child, in its relative lack of ability to coordinate and control its bodily movements and sensations, that experiences this fragmentation. Above all, in both neurotic and psychotic states of being, things fall apart. Psychopathology is based on the experience of fragmentation. In such a state, I feel myself 'coming apart at the seams,' 'pulled in all directions'; I feel powerless and out of control; I am 'breaking down.'

Lacan, in another article written about the same time as 'The mirror stage,' talked about the '*imagos of the fragmented body*,' images of 'castration, mutilation, dismemberment, dislocation, evisceration, devouring, bursting open of the body' that accompany the breakdown of the illusory identification with the ego (Lacan 1977b, p.13). It is as if the body were the battlefield on which the war of the subject with itself and others is conducted. Lacan cited the paintings of Hieronymus Bosch for their depiction of this *corps morcelé*, appearing in 'the form of disjointed limbs, or of those organs represented in exoscopy, growing wings and taking up arms for intestinal persecutions' (Lacan 1977b, p.5).

Breakdown in adult psychopathology represents a re-emergence of the fragmented bodily experience that the child marshals all its resources to avoid. And yet the alienating identification of the ego with its image is no more a cure for the adult than for the child. If I seek to captivate you with the image that I present, I will prevent you from ever coming to know me as I am. The question arises then, is there an experience of the 'I' that acknowledges the truth of its incompleteness yet is not experienced as aggressive disintegration? How can I experience the fragmented totality of my bodily being and not feel torn apart?

The claim I wish to make in this chapter, in opposition to Lacan's view, is that it is precisely through bodily expression that I can bear the suffering of my fragmented experience. The separation that Lacan makes between the imaginary of the body and the symbolic of speech itself needs to be deconstructed. In spite of his theoretical sophistication, Lacan seems to me to be still caught in the Cartesian dualism of mind and body. Although rejecting Descartes's concept of the ego as a substantial entity, a 'thinking thing,' he still locates subjectivity in opposition to bodily experience. The disembodied language of the psychoanalytic dialogue thus becomes a means of purifying the subject of its contamination by the body. For Lacan, the body itself can never be a locus of healing.

Without rejecting the insights that Lacan's critique of the ego has given us, we need to develop an account of bodily experience that will enable us to understand the positive meaning of bodily expression, even taking into account its chaotic character. Only such an account could make the effectiveness of expressive arts therapy comprehensible. I would like now to turn to the work of Maurice Merleau-Ponty as one source for such an approach.

In his book, *Phenomenology of Perception* (2002), Merleau-Ponty developed a phenomenology of the body that emphasizes the incarnate character of human existence. We are in the world not as disembodied consciousnesses but as beings that perceive the world through the senses. The body's lived experience of space and time outlines a horizon of being in which things have meaning for us. The French word *sens*, with its double meaning of sense and direction, indicates the extent to which the meaningfulness of the world arises out of our bodily movements. By virtue of my being a bodily subject, I am always situated in a specific time and place that is revealed to me through the direction in which I move. At the same time, I am continually transcending my concrete situation. Starting from where I am, I move to my destination. In so doing, I reveal the significance of my starting-place as well.

There is thus for Merleau-Ponty a fundamental or primordial experience of the body in which its capacity for transcendence is revealed. He called this *le corps propre*, the body that belongs to me or, we might say, my authentic bodily existence. The English translation of Merleau-Ponty's *Phenomenology of Perception* uses the phrase 'the lived body' to indicate the difference between this primary bodily experience and the body as objectified within a scientific framework. This latter concept of the body treats it as *partes extra partes* (elements disconnected from one another), a mechanical system lacking the intentional experience of being-in-the-world.

Furthermore, it is not only in scientific objectification that my body ceases to reveal itself to me as an originary starting-point. Merleau-Ponty reviewed the case studies of brain-damaged patients presented by Kurt Goldstein to show that in pathological cases the unity of bodily experience is what is most severely disturbed. Neurological impairment prevents patients from enjoying the bodily grasp of being; lacking a bodily sense of being here, they have to use their mental capacities to laboriously reconstruct their existential situation. (Oliver Sacks' studies of the effect of neurological damage upon perception seem to confirm Goldstein's and Merleau-Ponty's analyses: Sacks 1985.)

From this perspective, then, the fragmentation of the body that Lacan took as his starting-point assumes a new significance. Although the child lacks sensori-motor coordination, its experience is essentially different from a pathological one. The child is 'on the way' to a proper experience of its body. Its lack of coordination is an anticipation of a future state. Certainly this can be frustrating, as when the child's reach literally exceeds its grasp, but this frustration motivates it to keep moving in the direction toward which it aims.

Anyone who watches a child in its repeated attempts at standing can observe this phenomenon. Falling down for the child becomes an occasion for a renewed effort. Once achieved, the standing position can then be voluntarily relinquished, as falling down may become repeated as a form of play ('All fall down!'). The experience of the child in falling while learning how to stand is thus completely different from the experience of the child (or adult) who, once having learned how to stand, loses that capacity due to injury or illness.

It seems to me, therefore, that Lacan has projected back into the child's experience of its body the pathologies that are revealed in adult life. There is a difference between a unity that has broken down and one that has not yet been achieved. A shattered world is not the same as a world in the process of being formed. Of course, the child's world can also be destroyed, when trauma, for example, invades its fragile constitution; but such a situation cannot be seen as a necessary stage of development.

Merleau-Ponty's phenomenology of the body shows us the sea-change that occurs when the child's body takes hold of the world. This is the same accomplishment that accompanies any new configuration of being; to grow is to develop capacities that demand higher levels of coordination. For example, learning how to ride a bicycle or play an instrument requires a new way of coordinating my body. Once mastered, however, I now have this ability at my disposal; I can take it for granted without having to go through the learning process each time. Even after many years of disuse, my body 'remembers' the habitual movements involved in the exercise of a skill and can recover them with much less effort than was involved in the original learning experience.

The phenomenology of perception thus reveals the structures of behavior that enable me to achieve my goals in the world. At the same time, however, this instrumental behavior has not yet achieved expression. In order for the body to become expressive, it must do more than behave. It must signify; its behavior must mean something. Here is where Merleau-Ponty's thought has a special relevance for expressive arts therapy. Signification is not restricted for him to the linguistic sphere; rather, there is a primordial level of expression that takes place within the experience of the lived body. This primordial expression is contained in gesture.

Gesture stands midway between perception and language. It is a mute or indirect way of revealing the meaning of my situation. Although implicit in the act of perception, which, as we have said, already has a sense or direction, the gestural act aims not to accomplish a goal but to show the full meaning of what has been done. Gestures like waving goodbye, shrugging one's shoulders, raising one's hands in triumph, all call attention to the meaning of the situation in which I find myself. They are expressive gestures rather than instrumental acts (although they can, of course, be used instrumentally as well). The very posture of the body carries with it a wealth of expressive meanings, as I slump over dejectedly, stand proudly, contort my limbs in despair and so on.

Merleau-Ponty's notion of the expressiveness of gesture leads to the possibility of understanding artistic expression as well. We can call 'art' the gesture that goes beyond a mere indication of my situation and moves towards its transformation. Art is a gesture that transforms both self and world. By taking hold of my body in its various sensory modalities and motor capacities, I can expressively reveal the meaning of my situation and give it a new significance in terms of a possible future.

Ultimately, this means that art is not self-expression, at least not in the usual sense of that term. For Merleau-Ponty, it is clear that artists do not possess an inner self that they then have to translate into an outer form. Rather, the expressive act reveals a possible significance of the situation that previously lay hidden and unformed. By telling my story, for example, I do not repeat what I already know. Rather, I bring into being a latent and potential meaning that requires my assistance in order to be born. This is why, in genuine speech, I do not know what I am going to say until I say it. Certainly, I have an intention to say something, but what it is I have to say reveals itself to me as I go along. The same experience of not knowing what the result will be holds true in any process of art-making. There is therefore a certain risk in authentic expression; I can neither know nor control what will emerge.

The body speaks, whether directly or in the indirect language of the arts. But this speech is always addressed to another, another who is also a bodily being, situated in the world in the same way as I am. Therefore, in expression, the other must lend his or her own body to my significance; the other must be willing to go beyond or transcend his or her own situation in the direction that I indicate. Thus, not only do I risk revealing an aspect of myself of which I am ashamed, but also I run the risk of being misunderstood by the other. I can only hope that the other will meet me in the imaginary space of the expressive act. The therapist's role is, therefore, to be a witness to my expressive act, a witness who can testify to the significance that this act brings into being.

This testimony is itself expressive. The illusion of the therapist as a pure mirror to the client's expression cannot be sustained as soon as we take into account the therapist's own embodiment. The lived body of the therapist is called into question by the client's act of expression. Such an act requires a living response, an answer to a call. This is why feedback is so important in expressive arts therapy, not as reflection but as response. When the client's painting is answered by the therapist's poem, for example, they meet within an imaginal space full of meaning.

It seems to me that the role of the therapist in expressive arts therapy has to be rethought from the ground up, beginning with an understanding of the roots of expression. Otherwise, arts therapists will operate on the basis of a conception of the therapeutic relationship in which the expressive element is only an afterthought. Then the art in therapy will be a mere representation of an inner psychological state, a representation that has no special claim to validity and certainly no transformative power.

Just as the therapeutic relation assumes a new significance from the point of view of the lived body, so too does the expressive act. It is a mistake to think of the latter in analogy to the visual image of the mirror phase described by Lacan. In that description, we recall, the child avoids its fragmented being by taking refuge in the illusory identity of the image of its body. In this sense, identification with the mirror image, as well as with the gaze of others, is an inauthentic act; such identification uses the imaginary as a means of escape. In contrast, artistic expression takes up again the discordance of the human situation and gives it a new voice. Thus, Bosch does not paint idyllic pastoral scenes but, rather, directly confronts the violence and suffering endemic in his historical epoch. We could say that one of the bases of the expressive act in art consists of the revelation of human suffering and diremption. This is what enables the arts to be therapeutic. In expressive arts therapy, the capacity of human beings to find a form for their suffering is brought into play. Only on the basis of an authentic expression of clients' fragmentation can images of wholeness arise that are grounded in their situation as ideal horizons. Beauty is not contained within an image that brings us peace by veiling the horror of our situation. Rather, beauty, as Rilke reminded us, 'is nothing but the beginning of terror, which we still are just able to endure' (1984b). Unless we are able to endure the terror, we will have no access to beauty at all.

In expressive arts therapy, therefore, the body speaks, dances, sings and enacts scenes not in order to deny its fragmentation but to reveal it. Such revelation is also a transformation, a gathering up of the disjointed parts into a unity of signification. This unity forms what we might call a 'fragmented totality,' a way of being a self that neither falls apart into difference nor escapes into an idealized identity.

Merleau-Ponty does not imagine that the unity of expressive meaning reveals a fundamental harmony in our existence. For him, existence is always 'ambiguous' and chaotic: 'ambiguity is not some imperfection of consciousness or existence, but the definition of them' (Merleau-Ponty 2002, p.298) Since I am in the world as a lived body and not as a thinking thing, I can never find a stable place outside of the world from which I could survey my existence and master it in thought. However, I do not experience the ambiguity of existence primarily as pathological. There is a chaos intrinsic to my being and to that of the world which is the source of the multiplicity of significance that belongs to any act.

Moreover, this 'productive chaos,' as we might name it, is a possible way to come to terms with the fragmentation that stems from traumatic suffering. Since we *are* chaotic, we can face the chaos of trauma without feeling that we must expel it from our being. What we need to find then are the forms that can hold fragmentation. 'Healing' (if we choose to retain the word) in expressive arts therapy implies the acceptance of fragmentation as a permanent feature of human existence. We are always falling apart, and we always have an opportunity to come together if we have the courage to embrace our chaos rather than try to escape it. The bodily expression of being is the basis of the therapeutic power of expressive arts therapy. If we can accept the fragmented totality of our existence, we may have an experience of wholeness that will not be an escape into an idealized unity but will instead do justice to the nature of our chaotic and ambiguous being in the world.

8

# The Second Coming

## *Beauty, Chaos and the Arts*

Traditionally, beauty is thought of in conjunction with notions of order, harmony and proportion. Why then introduce this word, 'chaos,' between beauty and the arts? What is chaos? Why is it important for us to pay attention to chaos today? And what is the significance of this phenomenon for expressive arts therapy? These are the questions I would like to address in this chapter.

I would like to begin with the words from Yeats' 'The Second Coming,' to which I keep returning, *'Things fall apart; the centre cannot hold.'* Yeats' poem was written soon after the First World War, with the mass carnage in the trenches still vivid in the minds of Europeans. But the poem also presages events to come: the loosing of a 'blood-dimmed tide' and the inability of people of good will to find a foundation for their resistance to evil.

'The Second Coming' is a description of a certain kind of chaos: that of 'mere anarchy.' In this anarchic world, everything is disintegrating; no one can hold it all together. As the poem says, 'The falcon cannot hear the falconer'; nothing keeps the bird of prey from random destruction. The falconer is no longer the 'master'; he stands helplessly by while the forces he has unleashed upon the world act at will.

In this account of chaos, there is no connection between the parts of a chaotic totality. In a structured whole, on the other hand, the connection would ordinarily be maintained by a central power. This power, or ruling element, is one of the parts; but at the same time it governs the others. It is the 'master' part; the whole is under its rule. Just as in a political state the ruler or Prince holds the polity together, so in any ordered system, it would seem, there is a principle of rule in which a central element dominates the whole and organizes the parts into a meaningful and orderly totality.

A good example of this traditional conception of order and chaos can be seen in Plato's *Republic*. The just state that is constructed in Socrates' discourse is a hierarchical one in which the lower is subordinated to the higher. Farmers and artisans form a lower class ruled by the guardians, the soldier-watchmen who defend the state from internal and external enemies. At the top is the philosopher-king who commands the *polis*, the city-state, in the same way a captain commands a ship. A state ordered in such a way is deemed to embody 'excellence,' *arete* – a Greek word meaning both beauty and virtue.

Order in the state, for Plato, is modeled after order in the soul. *Polis* and *psyche* go together. Just as the wisdom of the philosopher-king, with the aid of the guardians, governs the workers, so the rational part of the soul should command the appetites, with the aid of the spirited or courageous and disciplined part. In *The Republic*, Plato outlines a conception of order that has been maintained in Western culture until the present day: reason must rule, else 'mere anarchy' will be loosed upon the world.

This conception accounts for Plato's attitude toward the poets. As we have noted, in classical Greek culture, education, *paideia*, was carried out through training in the arts. The poets were thus seen as the bearers of culture. In the oral tradition, the bard carried the story of his people from city to city, recounting, in such tales as the *Iliad* and the *Odyssey*, the legends and myths of the ancestors of the tribe. The tragic poets carried on this tradition in the great dramatic festivals dedicated to Dionysos. In classical Greece, poetry and education, *poiesis* and *paideia*, were one (Havelock 1963).

In *The Republic*, however, what Plato called 'the ancient quarrel between the philosophers and the poets' was initiated on a political level. The poets, says Socrates, are madmen; their souls are disordered. They know nothing of reason but are ruled by their passions. Their words stir men and women up and make them lose control of themselves. These madmen must be barred from the just city, for fear of infecting others with their disorder. The only acceptable poems are praises of the gods and stories of men who are just. These will calm the souls of the citizenry and lead them to emulate the orderly ways that are presented in verse.

Of course, Plato's own relationship to poetry is more complex than this doctrine suggests. The Platonic dialogues themselves are masterpieces of literary art; they embody both poetic vision and the charged and metaphoric language of art. The dialogue situation itself is a dramatic device. And several of the greatest dialogues, including *The Republic*, end not with argument but with myth. Plato implicitly concedes that there are limits to reason when he couches his answers to the ultimate questions of the fate of the soul and the nature of the gods in mythical form.

Nevertheless, the Platonic conception of order has become standard for Western thought. In this conception, order is thought to be hierarchical. The principle of order is embodied in a ruler who commands the other parts of the whole. This ruler is the center of the system around which the other parts revolve. If the rule of the center is challenged, then chaos will ensue. Chaos, therefore, is ugly and evil; only order can embody beauty and goodness. Reason and science are seen as ways towards the discovery of order; art and imagination lead to chaos and madness. If art is put in the service of order by following the rules of harmony and proportion, then it can have a useful subsidiary role in education. But art in itself has no principle of order; it must be ruled by reason or it will turn into chaos.

The understanding of modern science until recent times has followed this Platonic conception of reason and order. Here, nature is seen as an orderly system; its laws can be clearly grasped through mathematical structures. In principle, everything can be understood rationally; what does not exhibit systematic order is ultimately an illusion. Only order truly exists.

This vision of rational order was initially developed in an optimistic fashion. In the modern era, reason and order were envisioned as replacing superstition and tyrannical rule. The Enlightenment saw rationality as the motor for human liberation. Reason would bring freedom for human powers. The modern bourgeois state would be based on a 'civil society' in which the different social classes would each receive their just reward. The apparatus of the state would coordinate conflicting interests and ensure equitable treatment under the law. Ultimately, order in the state was to be based upon autonomy in the individual. The self-governing citizen would be capable of making decisions based on his enlightened self-interest. A well-functioning modern state requires autonomous individuals to bring about social harmony.

This vision of order and harmony was challenged strongly by the poet William Blake, who viewed the industrial revolution's 'dark Satanic

mills' as putting an end to the innocence of the agrarian community
(Blake 1977b, p.514). Blake saw clearly the connection between the
tendencies of the new science and the functioning of the emerging
capitalist order:

> For Bacon and Newton sheathed in dismal steel, their terrors hang
> Like iron scourges over Albion. Reasonings like vast Serpents
> Infold around my limbs, bruising my minute articulations
> I turn my eyes to the Schools & Universities of Europe
> And there behold the Loom of Locke whose Woof rages dire
> Washd by the Water-wheels of Newton; black the cloth
> In heavy wreathes folds over every Nation; cruel Works
> Of many Wheels I view, wheel without wheel, with cogs tyrannic
> Moving by compulsion each other: not as those in Eden: which
> Wheel within Wheel in freedom revolve in harmony and peace.
>
> *(Blake 1977a, p.661)*

This bleak view of the new emerging social order was echoed later
by Max Weber, who warned of the 'iron cage' of Western civilization,
based on what he called an 'inner-worldly asceticism,' the denial of the
senses, desire and the body (Weber 2003). In a famous passage toward
the end of *The Protestant Ethic and the Spirit of Capitalism*, Weber (2003)
refuses to predict what will become of our society:

> No one knows who will live in this cage in the future, or
> whether at the end of this tremendous development entirely new
> prophets will arise, or there will be a great re-birth of old ideas
> and ideals, or, if neither, mechanized petrifaction, embellished
> with a sort of compulsive self-importance. (2003, p.182)

Later in the century we can see in the work of Georg Lukács, *History and
Class Consciousness* (1972), and in the writings of the Frankfurt School of
Critical Theory, a continuation of this pessimistic assessment of Western
rationality, now spread to every dimension of human life, including the
innermost workings of the psyche. Herbert Marcuse's *One-Dimensional
Man* (2006) portrayed a society in which even the consciousness of an
alternative was lost. Logic and rationality rule; whatever cannot be the
subject of administration has no right to exist. The voice of Big Brother
in George Orwell's *Nineteen Eighty-Four* (1990), omniscient, omnipresent,
is taken as the model of authority. The center holds but with such a
tight grip that it chokes out all life from the body politic.

At the same time as the iron cage of Western rationalism becomes stronger, there are the beginnings of resistance movements, attempts to create alternative visions of reality. Friedrich Nietzsche is the prime example of such a creative resistance. When Nietzsche proclaimed that 'God is dead,' he foresaw the death knell of all centralized, hierarchical forms of order. In *The Birth of Tragedy* (originally titled, *The Birth of Tragedy out of the Spirit of Music*), Nietzsche (1967) contrasted the dominant rationality with an artistic vision of the world. His own thinking in this book was carried out within the form of myth: by employing the images of Apollo and Dionysus to embody the rational and the instinctual forms of life respectively, Nietzsche revived the ancient quarrel between philosophy and poetry, this time from an artistic perspective. Apollo, as the principle of order, justice, law and the autonomy of the individual, is contrasted with Dionysus, the god of festivity, the grape, orgiastic revelry and the Bacchanalian throng. Dionysus, we might say, is a god of chaos; and, as we have paraphrased a famous remark of Nietzsche's, 'you must have chaos within you to give birth to a dancing god.'

In this early work, Nietzsche re-visioned tragedy as a unity of Apollonian and Dionysian impulses. The Dionysian chorus, with its song and dance, lays the basis for the Apollonian hero, who speaks in measured verse. Without this basis in music, tragedy loses its ground and falls under the sway of Socratic dialectic. Philosophy itself, in the person of Socrates, is seen as a purely Apollonian form; only a revival of the Dionysian spirit can reconnect philosophy with life.

Nietzsche is a complex thinker whose own destiny led inexorably to madness as he descended into 'mere anarchy.' Nevertheless, his thinking is one of the first attempts to come up with a new conception of order – one that can admit the tendencies towards disorder inherent in life, yet also find a way to contain them. In Freud's writings, we see a parallel conception in the discovery of the unconscious. Freud, who remained a man of the Enlightenment throughout his life, was nevertheless fascinated by the discovery of a region of human existence that is not subject to the laws of logical non-contradiction. The disorder of the unconscious seemed to Freud to be the major factor in psychological life. Psychoanalysis, for him, became a method of restoring order in the psyche. 'Where *it* was, there *I* shall be,' became Freud's watchword. The goal of psychoanalysis, in Freud's view, is to replace the chaos of unconscious mental life with the order provided by the rational ego. Understanding the causal determinants of psychological behavior will show that within the chaos of the unconscious lies a potential hidden order, one which, when comprehended by consciousness, will manifest itself as more orderly or 'tamed.'

Psychoanalysis has always been ambivalent with regard to the unconscious. On the one hand, Freud never gave up hope that there could be a strictly rational science of mental life, that ultimately even the unconscious could be understood in terms of the physiological functioning of the organism. On the other hand, he knew that analysis was 'interminable'; he came to see with increasing clarity the fundamental irrationality of human existence and the incapacity of the energy of the instincts ever to be completely 'bound.' This ambivalence is part of the strength of psychoanalysis. It is able to hold on to both order and chaos, science and the unconscious. And its ambivalence has been seminal in generating intellectual tendencies as diverse as surrealism, on the one hand, and biological reductionism, on the other.

However, psychoanalysis in its classic form remains limited by its conception of rationality as antagonistic to chaos, in other words, by its roots in Platonic thinking. This conception leads to a notion of the psyche that is quite similar to Plato's. The ego is to rule in the soul; order in the psyche means the hegemony of a centered consciousness. The imagination must be kept under the rule of the central ego, or neurotic fantasies will gain predominance. In spite of Freud's own cultured tastes, he ultimately saw the artist as a failed scientist. The artist creates without awareness; his work requires the knowledge of psychic life attained by the analyst to be understood. Interpretation, then, becomes the method for finding the true (unconscious) meaning of the work.

Psychoanalytic thinking has developed in several directions since Freud. Ego psychology, for example, focused on the cognitive and volitional aspects of conscious life. The autonomy of the ego was seen as the goal of personal development. On the other hand, object-relations theory stressed the complex, chaotic nature of the unconscious and the importance of fantasy. D.W. Winnicott, in particular, tried to give a role to the notion of 'formlessness' as central in the development of the self. 'Formlessness,' in Winnicott's thinking, implies just letting experience be, without attempting to control or understand it (2005, p.45). In Winnicott's view, the child needs a care-giver to let him or her be, to tolerate his or her merely existing without having to be anything in particular. A care-giver who views the child as an extension of his own needs will force him to assume a particular shape in order to be loved. This 'false self' will then be experienced by the child as a mask necessary to ensure his survival (Winnicott 2005, p.19). However, at the same time, the child will have a sense of inner emptiness, of not really existing at all.

In the analytic situation, then, Winnicott strives to tolerate his patients' formlessness, their exisiting without a particular goal or pattern. Although in other circumstances Winnicott himself is a 'master' at interpretation, he nevertheless cautions against the interpretation of formlessness; such interpretation can reflect the analyst's anxiety about not knowing what is going on. At the same time, it cuts the patient off from contact with the unconscious and forces her to defend herself by splitting a true from a false self.

Another name for formlessness for Winnicott is 'play.' Play is the activity in which boundaries are transgressed. The child at play inhabits a transitional space in which he or she is neither one with nor separate from the other. 'Transitional space,' 'formlessness' and 'play,' it seems to me, are all ways of comprehending what we have called 'chaos.' For Winnicott, then, chaos is not to be mastered ('organized chaos is a denial of chaos') (Winnicott 2005, p.95). Rather, both the analyst and the patient must be willing to enter into the chaos of the psyche in order to arrive at a creative sense of self. Winnicott has the faith that there is an order within chaos, not a rational but an imaginal order. It is the order of play, art and creativity.

James Hillman's archetypal psychology similarly envisions a playful, creative psyche in which the imagination is the key to pattern, meaning and order. Hillman sees what Blake called Newton's 'single vision' as itself a form of fantasy, the fantasy of a heroic ego who aims to master reality. Hillman suggests that this fantasy is an unconscious one, since it is ignorant of its nature as fantasy. Once we see science itself as metaphor (the metaphor of a non-metaphorical reality), then we can be free from its mastery and able to engage in the imaginal workings of the psyche, no matter what form they take.

Part of Hillman's re-visioning of psychology is directed against the dominance of the ego. The ego, for Hillman, is another name for the hero. It operates through will, the will to power over self and others. Furthermore, the ego embodies a myth of isolation. The conquering hero who masters internal and external reality stands on the battlefield alone. He has slain all the monsters but as a consequence has only himself left to battle. Indeed, he will end by slaying himself as well. The male pronoun is appropriate here, since the image that is invoked is obviously a traditionally masculine one.

In opposition to this conception of the imperial ego, Hillman envisions a 'polytheistic' psychology, a conception of the psyche as inhabited by many archetypes and as serving many 'gods.' Thus 'multiplicity' becomes Hillman's way of imagining what we have called 'chaos.' The psyche, for Hillman, is multiple. It obeys no one principle of order, no one god. It is various in its manifestations. Nor do we need to impose order or unity upon it. Rather, in Hillman's view, if we can follow the multiple images of psychological life, we will be led further into what he calls 'soul.'

For Hillman, 'soul-making' is the goal of psychology. We make our souls by entering into their imaginal workings. As we come to inhabit and know each of our archetypal images, we will develop a richer and more variegated sense of ourselves. The poverty-stricken ego, embattled and alone, will be replaced by a community of celebrants, each offering something of value to their gods. Moreover, as we cease to identify with the isolated ego, our psychic life will become more communal, in the sense that we will come to see ourselves in others. We will recognize that we share certain primary fantasies, that we 'serve' the same gods. The world itself will become en-souled, as Newton's single vision is replaced by communal and festive celebration. Ultimately, as Hillman says, Descartes's *cogito ergo sum* will be replaced by *convivo ergo sum* (I party, therefore I am) (Hillman and Ventura 1993).

I see both Hillman and Winnicott as leading towards a new psychology, one that can admit the element of chaos in the psyche. It is significant that both are 'artistic' psychologies. In both of them, the poetic imagination, *poiesis*, has a central role. *Poiesis*, as the act of meaning-making and self-making, stems from the imagination. Only if we are able to inhabit the imaginal will we be able to become real, that is, souls and selves. The paradox is that the more we try to eliminate or master imagination, the more we will feel ourselves to be only phantasms, 'ghosts in the machine,' to use the phrase of the philosopher Gilbert Ryle (2002, p.9).

Furthermore, it is only imagination that, in its variety, is capable of encompassing chaos. Reason always strives for the universal, the One. The rational, autonomous ego is impoverished in so far as it cannot accept the multiplicity of the psyche, its capacity to change form, even to be without form.

Does this mean that there is no room for reason or for the ego? Are we solely writing in praise of chaos and against order? This is a difficult question for any psychology that bases itself in the imagination and in art. I once received a letter from Michael Eigen, the psychoanalyst and author, who commented that 'I don't think imagination is the answer, since imagination can be evil, too (nothing like evil imaginings to poison a civilization).' This is an objection that has often been made to Nietzsche and applies to Hillman as well: if there is no principle of order, then is not one form as good as any other? Isn't an aesthetic psychology fundamentally immoral? After all, Fascism, too, objected to the 'iron cage' of Western civilization and envisioned a 'new world order' based on irrational grounds. Isn't the mass slaughter of the death camps a possible consequence of the triumph of chaos over order?

One way of answering this objection is to distinguish 'true' or 'false,' 'authentic' or 'inauthentic' imagination. Winnicott makes a strong distinction between 'imagination' and 'fantasy' (Winnicott 2005, pp.36–37). 'Fantasy' in this sense is not creative; it has an obsessive, repetitive quality to it. Ultimately, for Winnicott, fantasy is a defense against existence; it is incapable of arriving at creative or symbolic form. This distinction between two forms of imagination is a traditional one, already made by Coleridge, and it has some validity. Among other things, it explains the difference between art and madness. The fantasies of the insane are not like those of the artist, though they may seem to be. Rather, madness is often over-ordered; instead of a productive chaos, there is a rigid set of recurring themes and beliefs, obsessive thoughts, paranoid ideas, symptomatic acts. There is no 'play' in this kind of fantasy, no capacity to relax and be, to let the images find their own diverse ways, to develop themselves into new emergent forms. Something similar can be seen by looking at Hitler's fantasies: his obsessive hatred of the Jews and other 'impure' elements of society, his belief in the Master Race, fated to rule others by the force of the will, his inability to imagine alternatives, even when the situation demanded it – all of these are signs of Hitler's being under the sway of fantasy rather than imagination. Imagination is free, not obsessive; multiple, not single-minded; variable, not constant and repetitive. If Fascism is a creature of the imagination, it is a monstrous one, not a true birth.

Having said this, there still remains the question: what enables imagination to distinguish itself from fantasy? Is there a rational component to the imagination that saves it from itself? Is there order in chaos? We have, following Winnicott, used the metaphor of play to understand imagination. If we read H.G. Gadamer's classic account of play in *Truth and Method* (2004 [1975]), we can see that he takes as the distinguishing feature of play its quality of being 'to-and-fro.' When I enter into the mode of play, I must relinquish mastery. I cannot stand outside as an isolated subject; rather, I must let myself be played by the back and forth movement of the game. This back and forth motion of play is in opposition to goal-directed movement. It is what Heidegger calls 'whiling,' tarrying in being. This is why play is so refreshing: I escape temporarily from the onward march of life, time seems to stand still, and for a while death itself is held in abeyance. Play is a formative category for Gadamer: he roots the essence of understanding and of language in the back and forth of play. In a genuine conversation, just as in a game, the participants forget themselves, let themselves be taken over, and finally arrive at a new position.

In a productive discussion, however, something new emerges which cannot be accounted for solely by the notion of play. There is an element of form or structure which appears when something new is discovered. This element is what separates play from art. Although for Gadamer art is rooted in play (as it is for Winnicott), in art there is an essential difference: playing gives way to 'transformation into a structure' when it becomes art. In this way, something new is created. This new form has a relative autonomy and integrity that enables it to be repeated. The possibility of performance itself depends upon the transformation of play into a structure.

Similarly, the 'self' of Winnicott has the characteristic of a relatively stable and permanent being; it is always in process, but it does not start from scratch each time. There is a 'building-up' of the self that enables the person to form stable relationships and follow through on commitments. With Hillman, it is not so clear that the soul has anything substantial about it. Yet what is 'soul-making' if it does not build or create anything that lasts? Even if it is primarily the quality of 'depth' that characterizes the soul and not permanent character traits, this depth can still only come through certain continued experiences. Otherwise the soul would become a narcissistic sampler of life's delights. It would be a butterfly soul, ungrounded and with no depth at all.

For a chaotic psychology to be possible, chaos must find an order of its own. Let us attempt to understand what kind of order this could be.

Gadamer recalls an example that Aristotle gives in trying to account for the formation of universal concepts out of particular experiences:

> Aristotle...says it is the same as when an army is in flight, driven by panic, until at last someone stops and looks around to see whether the foe is still dangerously close behind. We cannot say that the army stops when one soldier has stopped. But then another stops. The army does not stop by virtue of the fact that two soldiers stop. When does it actually stop, then? Suddenly it stands its ground again. Suddenly it obeys the command once again. (Gadamer 1977, p.14)

This example is interesting on many grounds. The army is in chaos. There is no order to its retreat. Suddenly an order is formed. How does this happen? Gadamer wants to show that this is the same way in which meaning occurs in our everyday experience of the world, as an immanent creative act of understanding. However the example seems to have been chosen by Aristotle for opposing reasons. The army is said to have obeyed its command once again; but can anyone seriously think that an army in rout will stop at a general's command?

The example reminds me of Tolstoy's depiction of warfare in *War and Peace* (1869). The generals give the orders, then the war happens in its own way (we might say, in a 'chaotic' way). Afterwards, the generals congratulate themselves on their prescience. It is interesting that concept-formation, which can also be considered, following Gadamer, as transformation into a structure, is modeled on a military analogy. As if experience obeys our commands! As if knowledge were an act of violence against the multiplicity of the self! At least the army was in retreat. This gives us hope for Aristotle, if not for his student, Alexander the Great.

In a later text (Michelfelder and Palmer 1989), as part of a debate with Jacques Derrida, Gadamer repeated his notion of the development of understanding, again citing Aristotle, in the latter's description of the 'freezing of a liquid when it is shaken as a *schlagartigen Umschlag*, a sudden reversal that comes like a blow from without.' Gadamer says this is similar to 'the blow-like suddenness of understanding, as the disordered fragments of the sentence, the words, suddenly crystallize into the unity of a meaning of the whole sentence' (Michelfelder and Palmer 1989, p.48). I would agree with this description of the sudden emergence of meaning. The transformation into structure comes all at once; we can never predict its occurrence. It is like the experience of insight or enlightenment. But it seems to me that the blow from outside, like the command of the general, is not the ruling principle, the factor creating order out of 'mere anarchy.'

I think Gadamer is relying here too much on the experience of the audience and not enough on that of the maker of the work. In encountering a genuine art-work, we are indeed struck as if by a 'blow from without.' But in making the work, there is no such external force. Rather, the work seems to form itself from within. Furthermore, as Gadamer himself indicates, transformation into a structure (*Gebilde*) is a mode of self-transformation (*Bildung*). We form ourselves through our creative experience. The form 'obeys' (if that is the correct word) an inner 'principle' of development. It is the 'product' of a 'process,' inextricable from the process itself.

Perhaps this is the link between play and art. I let myself play with the materials, immerse myself in them and give myself over to them. As I do so, their chaotic fragmentation begins to order itself. I can follow this order, mark it out and help it to emerge. It is like Winnicott's (1989) 'squiggle game,' which he used to play with children. Each partner draws a line, then the other partner must follow it. Out of the chaotic squiggles, order begins to emerge. Form comes from formlessness. Playing, whiling, dwelling in formlessness, are stages on the path to art-making. The pure repetition of the to-and-fro movement begins to point toward an emergent structure, a new creation of meaning.

The important point here is that order emerges out of chaos; it is not imposed from without. Nor does this order have the ruling character of the traditional ordering principle. No violence is done against the particulars, the fragments of the self. Rather, there is a trust that these fragments will eventually cohere into a new form, certainly not a permanent and unalterable one, but a form nevertheless.

This point of view can help us come to terms with Hillman's critique of the paradigm of development and growth. Hillman sees development as ego-building, the heroic ordering of experience. Consequently, in his opposition to the pre-eminence of the will, Hillman (1996) goes so far as to reject the whole notion of development. However, it seems to me that while it is true that development is *Bildung, paideia, poiesis*, that is to say, transformation into form and structure, this structure does not have to be a mandated, controlled and enforced pattern imposed from without. We may engage in 'soul-making' and shape ourselves in the same way as we engage in creative work: by letting the new form emerge without controlling it. We can neither control nor predict what we may be, but we can 'let ourselves be,' allowing new modes of selfhood to emerge. Personal development and growth come not from the mastery of experience, but from its playful transformation into form.

In the second stanza of Yeats 'The Second Coming,' the 'mere anarchy' described earlier leads to a revelation. The poet receives an image, a new form emerging into awareness: out of the chaos of our time a new being will emerge, a 'rough beast' which 'Slouches towards Bethelehem to be born.' It is the long-awaited second coming of the Messiah, but this time in the shape of a monster, a 'rough beast' whose terrifying aspect promises us not peace but nightmare. Almost a century after Yeats' poem was published, we know some of the forms that that 'rough beast' has taken. But is it not at least possible that chaos will give birth to a dancing god as well? Only if chaos is seen as the enemy of order must it appear in monstrous form. The order arising out of chaos, on the other hand, may well emerge as divine.

We do not know, nor can we predict or control, what form will emerge out of the anarchy of our era. But we can hope, and we can imagine that this time, when the army stops, it will do so with the awareness that the generals' commands are irrelevant, that we have created our own destinies, and that there will always be more surprises along the road.

In my mind's eye, I can see the army stopping. What happens next? Does it obey orders, turn and fight again? Does it stand still, mute and ashamed? Does it seek to embrace its enemy and make common ground against those in the rear who give the orders? Or does it leave the battleground, join the festivities and come to play the game of turning chaos into art? In that case, chaos will have found an order of its own, a new structure which can be performed again and again.

This can happen only if we learn to tolerate the anxiety which chaos brings, to wait while a new totality is forming itself out of the fragments. Chaos is the mother of all beings. We should not violate her by forcing a premature birth but rather learn to wait until her time is near. Then we can act and be of service. The therapist as artist is a midwife to the soul. Out of the soul's womb a new birth of forms can occur. Not with the forceps of the intellect but with the gentle hands of the imagination will we be able to assist this birth. Then perhaps the Second Coming will be an occasion not for despair but for joy.

# 9

# The Art of Despair

## *Therapy after Godot*

'Who lives in hope, dies in despair' (*Chi di speranza vive disperato muore*). This old Italian folk-saying reminds us that hope is an attitude that can lead us astray: when we spend our time waiting for a future that never comes, then we run the risk of ending with nothing at all. We will have never lived in the present, so our past crumbles into nothingness; it was only a series of expectations, an anticipation of something that never arrived.

On the other hand, can we live without hope? Dante's Hell has engraved over its portals: 'Abandon hope, all ye who enter here.' Thus it seems that to live without hope is to enter a sort of living Hell. Each moment would then remind us that we are without remedy, that nothing will save us from the meaningless passage of time, ending in death. We cannot live like that. Hope is as much a part of the human condition as its opposite, despair. We cannot avoid either the one or the other. Perhaps what we need to find is the kind of hope we can live with that does not end in despair. Is there what we might call an 'authentic' hope, a hope that is proper to being human? Immanuel Kant once said that there are only three questions worth thinking about: What can I know? What should I do? And what may I hope for? This last question is our topic here: What is the appropriate form of hope in our time?

It seems to me that Samuel Beckett addresses precisely this question in *Waiting for Godot* (1970). The play shows two characters, Vladimir and Estragon, who are waiting for Godot to come. Their entire hope is based on his coming, yet each day he sends a messenger to tell them that he will not arrive today but will surely come tomorrow. Vladimir and Estragon then have to pass the time until the next day, when they will see whether this time he appears.

It is too reductive to say that Godot is God, although the letters of the Almighty's name are contained within those of Godot. First, remember that the play was written originally in French, and '*Dieu*' forms no part of 'Godot.' Second, Beckett has said many times that if he knew who Godot was, he would have said so. And yet Godot is not 'not God' either. In fact, he bears a strong resemblance to our image of the Biblical patriarch. Godot is said to have a white beard; he treats his subjects in a mysterious way, rewarding some and spurning others for no obvious reason, and he demands an unthinking obedience. If he is not God, he is definitely 'like' God. Certainly, he serves this function in the lives of the characters: he is the one for whose coming they wait, the only one who can save them.

Godot is in fact like an absent god, a god whose absence defines the existence of those who wait for him. They have nothing to do except wait and hope that he will arrive. Each day they hope, and each night they despair. Thus they recapitulate the life-long cycle of hope and despair within the daily round of existence. Because they have nothing to do but wait, the question then arises, what to do while waiting?

The French title of the play is *En Attendant Godot* – that is to say, while waiting for Godot. What do we do while we wait for Godot to come or for night to fall? The play begins with an admission of the failure of the enterprise itself: the first line is, 'Nothing to be done.' There is nothing to be done that will be of any avail. We have no way of making Godot arrive; nothing we do, neither prayer nor good works, will compel his presence. Thus there is no reason to do anything. And yet we must do something; it is impossible for human beings not to act.

One solution is presented by the arrival of Pozzo and Lucky, who cross the stage and tarry for a while. They are going somewhere. Unlike Vladimir and Estragon, they have a purpose in life: Pozzo, the master, is taking Lucky, his slave, to market in order to sell him. Lucky is tied to Pozzo by a rope, somewhat like the way Didi and Gogo are tied to Godot. Pozzo is a man of importance: he possesses property and has power over another human being. And yet it does not take us long to see that Pozzo's solution is no better than any other. Pozzo's power is limited to the ability to make Lucky fetch and carry for him. When the two of them return in the second act, Pozzo has become blind and

Lucky dumb. Now Pozzo depends on Lucky; he has lost his sense of purpose and can only blindly say, 'On!'

The play shows clearly that the ordinary solutions of bourgeois life are of no help at all when it comes to the basic questions of existence. Power and property dissolve before the passage of time. So does intellect. When Lucky is asked to think, he does so in a chaotic 'word salad' which shows that his mind has completely deteriorated. What is interesting is that not only the content but also the very form of his speech show the same sense of deterioration and fragmentation. It is as if Lucky were a grotesque parody of the Kantian man of reason, the Enlightenment ideal. The intellect can no longer master reality; scientific understanding falls apart when faced with nothingness and death.

So we are left with Vladimir and Estragon, the two tramps. They are what the French call *clochards*, bums, former 'men of substance' who have fallen on hard times and have taken to the road. They no longer believe in bourgeois values, yet they are not artists either. They do not believe in the Romantic ideal of art as a means of salvation. At one point, Vladimir says, 'You should have been a poet.' In the text, Estragon replies, 'I was. (Gesture towards his rags.) Isn't that obvious?' Poetry will no more bring Godot than power will; both are purposeless forms of activity.

What then remains? Gogo and Didi play to pass the time. They engage in repartee, exchange hats, insult each other, even play at being Pozzo and Lucky. Since there is nothing to be done, they 'play' at doing; in fact, they are 'play-actors.' It is no accident that the word, 'play,' in both English and German (*Spiel*) has the double meaning of both child's play and theater. Actors in a theater are not real agents; they do not accomplish anything in the world. Rather, they 'play' at acting. Acting 'imitates' life, but the reverse is true as well, as Shakespeare reminded us. The stage can be a metaphor for reality: 'All the world's a stage.' There is thus a double equivalence between theater and life; they refer back to each other equally.

Yet Didi and Gogo are not Shakespearean actors – that is, they are not tragic heroes. If characters like them appear in Shakespeare at all, it is as the 'fools' who often reveal the truths of which their masters are ignorant. They remind us of Shakespeare's gravediggers, for whom death is the final, and perhaps only, joke.

In the first act, when Pozzo still is capable of accomplishing something, he makes as if to leave the scene, saying, 'But I really must be getting along, if I am to observe my schedule.' Vladimir responds, 'Time has stopped.' Pozzo, checking his watch, says, 'Don't you believe it, Sir, don't you believe it... Whatever you like, but not that.' But in the second act, when the now-blind Pozzo returns, and Vladimir asks him when Lucky became dumb, Pozzo answers furiously:

> Have you not done tormenting me with your accursed time! It's abominable! When! When! One day, is that not enough for you, one day he went dumb, one day I went blind, one day we'll go deaf, one day we were born, one day we shall die, the same day, the same second, is that not enough for you? (Calmer.) They give birth astride of a grave, the light gleams an instant, then it's night once more. (Beckett 1970)

The grave is the truth of time in *Godot*. We are born, we suffer, we die. The time between birth and death is an instant; it is no time at all. Later, Vladimir picks up Pozzo's theme: 'Astride of a grave and a difficult birth. Down in the hole, lingeringly, the grave-digger puts on the forceps. We have time to grow old. The air is full of our cries.'

Vladimir adds, 'I can't go on.' The recognition of the futility of life stops action. It runs the risk of stopping existence as well. But at that moment, the boy returns, the messenger of Godot. This time Vladimir has no expectations; his hope has ended; he knows Godot will not come that evening. He ends his questioning of the boy by exclaiming, 'Christ have mercy on us!'

Yet when the boy asks, 'What am I to tell Mr. Godot, Sir?' Vladimir responds, 'Tell him...tell him you saw me and that...that you saw me.' Futile or not, our existence demands a witness. Just as the actors must be seen by the audience in order to exist, so human beings in general need a witness to verify their being. Even if all we are capable of is suffering, yet that suffering demands an other to see it: not to save us from our suffering but to acknowledge it as the truth of our being.

Didi and Gogo play to pass the time, but they play in front of an audience. They do not play to entertain the audience; they are not 'crowd-pleasers.' They know that the audience cannot save them. At one point, when they think that they are going to be attacked, the two tramps look for a refuge. Vladimir pushes Estragon toward the audience, and when Estragon 'recoils in horror,' Vladimir says, 'You won't? (He contemplates auditorium.) Well I can understand that.'

Nor does Beckett think that *Waiting for Godot* will be a means of salvation for its audience either. The characters continually underline how meaningless their behavior is. (At one point, Vladimir remarks, 'This is becoming really insignificant.' To which Estragon replies, 'Not enough.') The characters cannot find salvation in art, and the play does not offer any such salvation to the audience. Yet *Waiting for Godot* is still art. It is theater without action (one critic said that *Godot* is a play in which 'Nothing happens. Twice.'), yet it is still theater. What does this play tell us about the possibility of art-making today?

If we take *Godot* seriously, then we can no longer pretend that we will be saved by art. Art no more brings salvation for us than does religion, with which it was once linked. And this for the same reason: We have looked into the heart of history and found what Kurtz found in *The Heart of Darkness*, 'The horror! The horror!' (Conrad 2001, p.137). We remember what Joyce (1998), who can be regarded as Beckett's 'master,' wrote in *Ulysses* 'History...is a nightmare from which I am trying to awake' (p.34).

The Holocaust, or Shoah, served as a symbol in the twentieth century for this incapacity to find salvation in historical time. In this regard I find something obscene about the success of such films as Steven Spielberg's *Schindler's List* (1993). In that film, the Holocaust became the subject of a Hollywood epic in which good triumphs over evil. The heroic individual defeats his evil nemesis, bringing justice to the community (or what remains of it), and then rides off into the sunset. Of course, I was 'moved' by the movie, as were countless others. The scenes of suffering, accompanied by a schmaltzy soundtrack, could not fail to move the audience to tears. It was truly a 'cathartic' experience, in the sense of an emotional bath.

Yet this is exactly what Beckett refuses. There is no artistic representation of the Holocaust that can provide a 'catharsis' in this sense. Such purification is no longer possible. We have been polluted beyond the capacity of heroic action. To watch *Schindler's List* is to be reminded of Adorno's warning (1983, p.34) that to write poetry after Auschwitz is barbaric.

*Schindler's List* is an example of the horrifying capacity of humans to forget history while seeming to honor it through memory. There is more of Auschwitz in Beckett than in Spielberg, in spite of the 'authenticity' of the survivors' memories that serve as the basis for his film. If we truly remembered the Holocaust, we would be silent, or else we would, with Beckett, present the despair that lies at the center of our hope.

It is no accident that during the siege of Sarajevo in the 1990s, Susan Sontag came to the Bosnian city to stage *Waiting for Godot*. The play was a repetition (*mimesis*) of the experience of the inhabitants: to wait, to be disappointed, to wait again, finally to realize that the one who is waited for will never arrive, to go on living while recognizing one's plight – this is exactly the atmosphere of *Godot*. Should we have sent the citizens of Sarajevo prints of *Schindler's List* instead? I can't even imagine it.

Beckett's art does not promise salvation; it offers suffering to be witnessed. In its recognition of the limits of art, it reminds me of Kierkegaard's *Either/Or* (1987). Kierkegaard's entire work is a sustained meditation upon the theme of hope and despair. Perhaps a comparison of Beckett with Kierkegaard here will serve to illuminate the meaning of *Waiting for Godot*.

The first volume of *Either/Or* purports to contain the papers of 'A', a young man who lives what Kierkegaard calls an 'aesthetic' way of life. In the first of his purported papers, the 'Diapsalmata' or 'Refrains,' addressed to himself, 'A' describes what a poet is:

> An unhappy man who in his heart harbors a deep anguish, but whose lips are so fashioned that the moans and cries which pass over them are transformed into ravishing music. His fate is like that of the unfortunate victims whom the tyrant Phalaris imprisoned in a brazen bull, and slowly tortured over a steady fire; their cries could not reach the tyrant's ears so as to strike terror into his heart; when they reached his ears they sounded like sweet music. And men crowd about the poet and say to him, 'Sing for us soon again' – which is as much as to say, 'May new sufferings torment your soul, but may your lips be fashioned as before; for the cries would only distress us, but the music, the music, is delightful.' And the critics come forward and say, 'That is perfectly done – just as it should be, according to the rules of aesthetics. (Kierkegaard 1987, p.19)

This is very close to Beckett, even in Kierkegaard's view of critics:

> Now it is understood that a critic resembles a poet to a hair; he only lacks the anguish in his heart and the music upon his lips. I

tell you, I would rather be a swineherd, understood by the swine,
than a poet misunderstood by men. (Kierkegaard 1987, p.19)

We recall that the great duel of insults in *Godot* between Vladimir and
Estragon ends only with the ultimate 'Crritic!' uttered by Estragon 'with
finality,' according to the stage directions.

'A' lives as a poet, which means, in Kierkegaard's view, that he
pursues pleasure but finds only despair. The first volume of *Either/Or*
takes us through the stages of aesthetic existence, beginning with the
'immediate stages of the erotic' which show the futility embodied in
the Don Juan myth, the search for sensual immediacy. The poet tries to
overcome despair through erotic love, but each conquest immediately
reveals itself to be insufficient, so he must begin again. This is what
Hegel called 'bad infinity' (2008, p.109), a process that not only never
ends but also never finds satisfaction.

From eroticism, the poet passes to doubt. Like Faust, he wonders if
he can ever say to the moment, 'Stay, thou art fair!' Finally, his doubt
becomes despair, as he realizes that he will never find the eternal in
history. Like the Wandering Jew, he is doomed to an unending search
without hope.

For Kierkegaard, then, it is not only that art cannot bring salvation.
He makes the stronger point that to pursue an aesthetic existence is to
end with an ultimate sense of despair. At the same time, Kierkegaard
welcomes this despair as opening up the possibility of choice. Aesthetics
lived to its limits brings the possibility of choosing one's own despair,
rather than seeking to avoid it. If we can choose ourselves in our despair,
in Kierkegaard's view, then we have the possibility of achieving an
ethical existence, one in which we are reconciled with the universal in
the form of morality.

Volume Two of *Either/Or* discusses the dimensions of that ethical
existence. It is written in the form of letters to 'A,' ostensibly penned
by Judge William, an older man who professes to find in marriage the
ethical solution to the problem of living a sensual life, given our existence
as temporal beings. By keeping the promise that we have made to each
other, the marital relationship brings eternity into temporal existence.
For Judge William, the aesthetic attitude is unable to see the beauty of
fidelity because it is compelled to represent experience as a series of
intensive moments. Artistic representation, in its concentration of the
passage of time into the significant moment, is incapable of presenting
the beauty of a long-term relationship that slowly ripens into bloom.

We will not go into the relationship of this theory to Kierkegaard's own life. It is clear that he struggled with the conflict within himself between the aesthetic and the ethical attitudes; in some way, the book can be read as a message addressed to Regina Olsen, the fiancée whom he had rejected out of a sense of shame over his own and his father's lust. Volume Two of *Either/Or* is an attempt to show that the choice of the ethical state of marriage can overcome the selfishness and despair of eroticism that make it shameful, and that it can also incorporate erotic impulses into a caring, joyful union. This was not an altogether convincing argument, either for Regina or for Kierkegaard's readers.

Part of the difficulty is that the tension between aesthetics and ethics, between individual expression and social obligation, seems to be eliminated in Judge William's letters. They lack the passion of 'A's writings, as well as their poetry. For this reason, they do not speak to the reader in a compelling way. Perhaps Kierkegaard is working against himself here: *Either/Or* is itself an 'aesthetic' work, as opposed to what Kierkegaard called an 'edifying' one, in which truth would be directly communicated without artistic representation. In *Either/Or*, the truth is presented through the contrasting images of the different stages of existence, that is, through art. *Either/Or* is art arguing against itself. If we are convinced, then we have simultaneously proven the opposite.

The situation is no better in *Fear and Trembling* (1985), Kierkegaard's other great 'aesthetic' work. Here Kierkegaard tries to remedy the limitations of the ethical emphasis upon the universal by imagining a call to go beyond duty. What he calls the 'teleological suspension of the ethical' is presented by the story of Abraham and Isaac, in which God calls upon Abraham to overcome his ethical obligations to his son and sacrifice him in God's name. Kierkegaard tells the story over and over again in different ways, in an attempt to understand how Abraham could have the faith to carry out such an incomprehensible task. In this case, unlike that of marriage as set forth by Judge William, there is no universal obligation compelling Abraham to act. Rather he must rely on a purely individual relationship to God that can be based only in faith.

*Fear and Trembling* shows that for Kierkegaard salvation comes ultimately not through ethical action but only through a 'leap of faith,' in which the finite human consciousness trusts that the eternal being holds us in his care. Without this faith, as Kierkegaard points out, Abraham could only be considered to be a monster.

Again, this argument seems unconvincing to us today. We need only remind ourselves that recent 'leaps of faith' (in which the ethical is suspended in obedience to God's commandments) have been the foundation for acts of violence and terror, in order to be assured that the religious solution is no more valid than the ethical one.

In fact, the greatness of *Fear and Trembling* rests not on its conclusions but on its manner of presentation. The book is a poetic re-telling of the Biblical myth, not an ethical argument or a religious treatise. The use of a pseudonym for the author's name again puts *Fear and Trembling* into the category of Kierkegaard's 'aesthetic' works. The book is purportedly written by *Johannes de silentio*, John of silence. The name indicates Kierkegaard's conviction that the truth cannot be communicated directly but only in an indirect manner. Here, then, we have an aesthetic presentation of the religious transcendence of the ethical. As powerful as the book is, I wonder if it can achieve its goal of stimulating religious conviction, or whether it, too, is limited to the power of art to represent faith imaginatively.

If, after this journey through Kierkegaard, we turn back to Beckett, perhaps we can see his work differently. Beckett refuses to leave the aesthetic; he acknowledges that his play is just a play and nothing more. Yet he does not see the aesthetic as an attempt to avoid despair, as Kierkegaard does. Rather, for Beckett, art today bears the responsibility of acknowledging the depth of our despair as well as the magnitude of our longing. As he once put it, he aims for an art that prefers, 'The expression that there is nothing to express, nothing with which to express, nothing from which to express, no power to express, no desire to express, together with the obligation to express' (Beckett 1965, p.103).

Thus we might say that, rather than Kierkegaard's image of art leading to a despair which can be overcome only through a leap of faith, Beckett imagines an art that embodies its own despair, that chooses, we might say, to live without the illusions of art. Beckett's art is similar to what might happen if the victims of the tyrant Phalaris, referred to in *Either/Or*, were to emerge from the brazen bull in which they were imprisoned and tortured. Their cries would then no longer sound like 'sweet music,' but rather exactly like what they are: the suffering of the damned. Would they then 'strike terror into the tyrant's heart?' And would men still crowd around the poet and say, 'Sing for us again?' Not to mention, would the critics consider these cries perfectly done, according to the rules of aesthetics?

Beckett promises an art without illusions; can we say, an art without hope? In spite of all, there is one hope left in Beckett, the hope in art to represent the hopeless. Not by finding a new form of faith, not by promising salvation in any form, but only by bearing witness to the truth of our time: 'The horror! The horror!' This is the art of the survivor. Not the victim-survivor, who finds a new faith in the resentment born of victimization. Rather it is the faith of Ishmael, cast out into the wilderness by Abraham, who reappears in *Moby Dick* to say, like Job, 'And I only am escaped alone to tell thee.' He is the sole survivor, whose mission is not revenge but becoming a witness to the truth of suffering.

What is remarkable in this theater, a theater not of poverty but of emptiness, is that the witnesses to the truth are not tragic heroes but clowns. Their suffering is lamentable, but also absurd; they retain none of the dignity of the classical hero. Rather, their comedy is visible in the disproportion between their situation and the means they have to cope with it. Kierkegaard himself saw the closeness of humor to faith. In Beckett, humor *is* faith, the faith that there is 'nothing to be done' but play.

At the end of this play about the meaninglessness of life and the unavoidability of death, Vladimir and Estragon try to hang themselves. They attempt to use the rope that holds up Estragon's trousers, but it breaks. In the course of this mock-suicide, Estragon's trousers fall down:

*Estragon*: Well, shall we go?

*Vladimir*: Pull on your trousers.

*Estragon*: What?

*Vladimir*: Pull on your trousers.

*Estragon*: You want me to pull off my trousers?

*Vladimir*: Pull ON your trousers.

*Estragon*: (realizing his trousers are down) True. (He pulls up his trousers.)

*Vladimir*: Well? Shall we go?

*Estragon*: Yes, let's go.

The stage directions then read: 'They do not move.'

There is nowhere to go, nothing to do, yet one thing we can do is what the clown does: we can drop our trousers and show ourselves to others. We can play together and witness the absurdity of our lives. It will not give us meaning or direction; we still cannot move. But it will help to pass the time. And it will make us laugh.

Perhaps laughter, for Beckett (as for Nietzsche), is the only saving grace. We laugh not at others but at our own suffering, the disproportion between our ends and our means. We who would taste eternity gleam for an instant and then pass into night. We are absurd and we know it. But still we demand to be witnessed. We make art not to be saved, but to be seen in all our incommensurability. Can we find a way to honor our mortality without turning it into myth? If the joke is on us, can we bear to tell it and, perhaps, even laugh?

If to live in hope is to die in despair, then perhaps to live in despair is to die in hope. By abandoning the myth of salvation, without surrendering the pathos of the infinite, we are given the divine gift of laughter by means of which we can witness our own condition. This is the message of Beckett's art of despair.

From the perspective of this book, then, we might ask, what are the implications of Beckett's art for the therapeutic enterprise? Is there the possibility of therapy after *Godot*? What remains when the promise of salvation is taken away?

*Godot* teaches us the limits of therapy as well as of art. It is difficult for therapists not to want to be healers. People come to us to be healed; they look to therapy for the end of their suffering. It is only too easy to believe in their image of us, to identify with the shamanic archetype: the one who has received the divine power to heal. But therapy cannot take away suffering. To think that it could would be a misunderstanding of the human condition. Psychopathology, the *pathos* of the *psyche*, is intrinsic to human being, as James Hillman never ceased to remind us. Any therapy that promises to eliminate suffering is itself pathological: it is unconscious of its own limitations (though, of course, one goal of therapy is to reduce *unnecessary* suffering).

This temptation is particularly strong, perhaps, for expressive arts therapists. For us, the therapeutic myth is coupled with the Romantic belief in the power of art to transform reality. This belief is no longer present in the same way in the actual practice of art, but it sometimes seems that it has migrated into the arts therapies. Thus the expressive arts therapist is tempted to believe that here at last art has fulfilled its original promise of transformation.

To say that expressive arts therapy has limits is not to say that it is worthless. But the first task in assessing its value is to become aware of these limits, or else client and therapist will end up collaborating in a mutual self-delusion. This task requires a certain 'ascetic' attitude applied to our own practice; we need to purify expressive arts therapy of the Romantic myth of art. This will, in turn, enable us to receive the gifts that the practice of art can bring.

The most important of these gifts is the capacity to be present. The practice of the arts requires presence above all else: 'being there,' in the emphatic sense. The openness and receptivity of this presence allows for images to enter our space. Presence makes imagination possible. The image itself is a messenger, an 'angel' in the original sense of the word. It announces itself as an unexpected gift from beyond, a visitor from another world. I can never compel its presence, but I can invite it and wait for its arrival. In this sense, the image is not like Godot; it will come, if I can learn to wait.

What is the relationship of the image to suffering in expressive arts therapy? The image is the face of our suffering; it is what shows itself when we look our suffering 'in the face.' In coming forth in all its ugliness, it achieves a paradoxical beauty that transcends the canons of aesthetics. In expressive arts therapy, we must take away the brazen bull that transforms the cries of the suffering psyche into beautiful illusion (*Schein*). Rather, if we can tolerate listening to these cries without shrinking away, we will hear the 'ugly beauty' that comes from the mouth of pain.

Heidegger (1975) has shown us that the 'creators' of works come into being only through the work's 'preservers.' In the same way that the practice of art requires the presence of an audience to receive the image that arrives, so the practice of expressive arts therapy requires that the therapist be present to witness the images that come to her client. The images do not ask to be fixed or changed; above all, they do not seek to be eliminated. What they require is a witness to their presence. Purifying expressive therapy of the Romantic myth of art does not take away the power of this work. On the contrary, this asceticism can bring about the full power of the therapeutic act: to be capable of responding to the suffering of another.

*Waiting for Godot* shows us the power of an art without illusions, but it does not thereby render art impotent. Rather, it demonstrates the essential capacity of art to express suffering. At the same time, the play shows us that suffering must have a witness. The players do not exist without the audience, Gogo and Didi do not exist without each other, and the essential thing about Godot is that he embodies the image of the one who sees everything and thereby sustains it in being.

Thus, although there is no salvation in *Waiting for Godot*, there is the possibility of being seen. Is anything more required of us as expressive arts therapists? All that is necessary is to be present to the suffering of others, to witness the face of that suffering in the images that arrive. This perspective does not take away the power of therapeutic art, but rather restores it to its rightful place: its capacity to be fully present. Our faith is that this presence is enough, that nothing more is required of us than to be attentive to the suffering of another. If we can do this, our hope will rest upon solid ground. For, as Rilke has told us,

> Only he whose bright lyre
> has sounded in shadows
> may, looking onward, restore
> his infinite praise.
> *(Rilke 1986, p.35)*

# 10

# Researching Imagination –
# Imagining Research

What is research in expressive arts therapy? As soon as we ask this question, we have stepped outside the realm of research itself. The question 'What is it?' is fundamentally a philosophical question, as Socrates showed. It cannot be answered by giving examples of the thing being asked about, for what we call a thing is not necessarily what it is. To understand the 'what' of something requires that we seek to understand its essence, that which makes it the thing it is. In this chapter, I would like to provide a philosophical perspective on the question of what research in expressive arts therapy is.

For Socrates, the question of the 'what' requires that we enter into a dialogue, that we follow the logos – the thought/meaning/reason/discourse that enables us to understand the essence of what we are asking about. *Dia-legein*, to follow the thought, means to let oneself be guided not by one's own interests but by that which we interrogate. 'Listen not to me, but to the *logos* within me,' said Heraclitus. And, similarly, Husserl (1982, p.35) advised us to go 'Back to the things themselves!' to let our thinking be guided by what is to be thought and not by our ideas about it. Phenomenology, then, can be seen as an explicit formulation of the Socratic maxim: we attempt to think that which shows itself to us, the *logos* of the phenomenon.

When we look at the question 'What is research in expressive arts therapy?' we see many examples of projects being carried out according to established scientific methodology. Whether the studies are quantitative or qualitative in nature, they follow procedures that are methodically established. Often, as Shaun McNiff points out in *Art-Based Research* (1998), the motivation of these studies is to justify the arts therapies in the eyes of other professionals, to establish that we are 'legitimate' and deserve to be accorded a place at the table of mental health professions. The motivation of a project should not in itself discredit it. Justification may be a valid motive; and, in any case, noble acts are often committed from base intentions. (Samuel Johnson, the great English man of letters, once declared, 'The man who does not write for money does not write for me.')

The problem with many of the current research projects in the arts therapies is that they lack imagination. They are as dry as dust. They lack the most important quality of that which they are investigating – the aesthetic dimension of our work, that which excites us, turns us on, makes our breath come faster: the erotic, dynamic vitality of our field. Heraclitus also said that everything is fire; the world is alive. The task of our thinking is to capture the aliveness of our being, to follow it and help it express itself in words.

One of the sub-themes of McNiff's book is the concept of 'energy': the imagination is energetic. Images possess energy, and they demand that we respond to them with the energy of our own imagination. If we try to think the image, we must find an imaginative, energetic way of thinking. Otherwise we will kill it: we murder to dissect. And in that case, we will turn against thinking itself. Socrates warned against 'misology,' the hatred of thinking. For him the danger came from sophistry, from those who taught their students to persuade others by rhetorical tricks, to make the weaker cause appear the stronger in public debate, and thereby to enable their interests to prevail.

For us today, the greater danger is that we will take for granted the conventional opinion that 'research' means following an established scientific methodology. We will thereby produce studies that no one will want to read and, on the other hand, we will allow thinking to be defined in a way that will make us see it as a danger to experience. Students habitually speak of expressive arts therapy as 'non-verbal therapy,' thereby not only neglecting the obvious verbal dimension of the arts (poetry, story-telling, drama), but also revealing the fear that to use language means to reduce the rich, creative field of sensible experience to an arid, logical plain, to turn the living into the dead.

It is interesting that in the Platonic dialogues themselves, the tension between image and word, imagination and thought, is maintained. Although in *The Republic* Socrates bans the poets from the just city because their images distort reality and stir the passions, thereby creating public disorder, nevertheless, as we have noted, the style of the book itself reveals its imaginative dimension. Thinking is carried out in the form of a dramatic dialogue, the main ideas are presented through metaphor, and the entire work ends with the recounting of a myth that purports to tell us about the nature of that which we cannot know by thought alone.

All the Platonic dialogues have an aesthetic dimension. Moreover, they are animated by a passionate and agonistic (even aggressive) thinking that stirs the reader, making his or her own thoughts come alive. After Plato, this aesthetic, imaginative dimension is largely lost in the Western concept of knowledge – or, perhaps, it is concealed in the sober analysis of logical discourse, living only as the engine that drives thinking to persist without being aware of its own motivating force.

It is not until Nietzsche's *The Birth of Tragedy* (1967) that we encounter a philosophical text that is suffused with the imaginative dimension. Nietzsche, trained as a classical philologist, eschews the scholarly apparatus of his time and engages creatively with his subject: the 'What is it?' of Greek tragic drama – the highest expression, in the opinion of his contemporaries, of art itself. German-language scholarship saw the greatness of tragedy in its language, the articulated expression of an orderly, harmonious way of being. The hubris (or overweening pride) of the hero creates a disorder in the cosmos that can be corrected only by his fall. The speech of the tragic characters is an attempt to restore order to the world.

For Nietzsche, on the other hand, the exclusive focus on the texts of the tragedies reveals a failure of scholarly imagination. Only the texts have been handed down; we read them as if they were literature, thereby neglecting their performative dimension, which is the essence of theater. If we imagine the texts being performed in front of an audience, we come, in particular, to understand the role of the chorus in a new way. The chorus does not engage in discourse; it dances and sings. Choral song and dance, far from being an impediment to the 'real' stuff of tragedy, the speech of the individual actors, is the very foundation of the art. Tragedy, for Nietzsche, arises out of communal song and dance; the measured speech of the protagonists takes place against this collective, bodily expression.

This vision of tragedy led Nietzsche to a more far-reaching perspective. He saw the whole of Greek culture, seemingly so harmonious and serene, as a response to a basic experience of the chaos of life. It is because life itself is chaotic, conflictual, passionate, even violent – in a word, alive – that the Greek tragic artists were able to forge works that embodied both the *eros* and the *logos* of existence. The greatness of Greek tragic drama – and indeed of all art – is in its ability to marry these two dimensions of our being.

Nietzsche embodied these two aspects of life in the images of two gods of Greek mythology: Apollo and Dionysus. Apollo, Socrates' patron, the god of light, of justice, of individuality and rational thought, is contrasted with Dionysos, the god of the underworld, of the vine, of communal revelry, suffering and redemption. The Apollonian and the Dionysian are the two great forces or principles of existence: order and chaos, mind and body, reason and passion, science and art – all the great antitheses of life are present in this imaginative conception. The strength of Nietzsche's vision lies not in a rejection of the Apollonian (this was the Nazi regime's deliberate misreading of Nietzsche's work). Rather its power consists in the realization that the Apollonian is only fully possible on the basis of the Dionysian, that *logos* depends on *eros*, and that we are in danger of creating a world in which the erotic dimension is denied. And since this dimension cannot ultimately be denied (as Freud understood when speaking of the 'return of the repressed') it will express itself blindly in self-destructive ways, above all by the desire to master existence by logic, a passion that may yet lead us to the destruction of the earth.

It would be well for expressive arts therapists to keep this Nietzschean vision in mind. If, in our research, we lose the Dionysian dimension of our work, we lose thereby its very foundation. The goal is not to obliterate oneself in a Dionysian orgy (though that may have its appeal when the alternative is a bureaucratized universe), but to harness the energetic dimension of aesthetic experience and join it to the articulate expression of artistic form. Art is always Apollonian – there is, as Majken Jacoby has put it, a 'necessity of form' (Jacoby 1999, p.53) – but form must have a dynamic basis in order to be alive, to seize us with the power of the gods.

Art-based research, then, needs to pay attention to both dimensions of our work. It must honor the demand for clarity, order, form, meaning, logic, and all the other dimensions of the Apollonian, but it must also embody the passionate, erotic, vital basis of the arts. If we ask 'Is this science?' we must be clear that we know what science is, that we do not take for granted an Apollonian conception of knowledge that would betray the very heart of what we seek to understand.

Hans-Georg Gadamer, in *Truth and Method* (2004 [1975]), contrasts the methodical procedures of scientific rationality with the capacity of art to reveal a deeper truth about human existence. For Gadamer, truth can never be reached by method. 'Truth,' for him (following Heidegger), is not mere correctness of correspondence to a pre-existing reality; rather, truth is the uncovering of the meaning of being. Such an uncovering demands that we enter into a dialogic relationship with that which we seek to understand, a relationship in which not only the being of the thing we study but also our own existence comes into question. The experience of a work of art is for Gadamer an archetype of the revelation of truth. To understand the work demands more than a detached objectivity. Rather, we confront the work with our own being, in a passionate encounter in which it speaks to us in a way that shatters our preconceptions.

From this point of view, a 'method' based on the detached observation of an objective state-of-affairs neglects our involvement in what we interrogate and runs the risk of reducing the phenomenon to what we already know. The truth that actually matters to us is the truth of our existence; to reach it requires that we put ourselves at stake in the enterprise of knowledge. This does not mean that we must be against 'science' – the controlled objectivity of scientific method is wholly appropriate to the objects which it interrogates. Otherwise, we would run the risk of prejudicing our understanding with our own point of view. Nothing could illustrate this better than Stalin's attempt to create a 'Soviet' science – the notion that 'nature' is different when seen from a socialist or any other particular perspective (feminist, post-colonial, etc.) is deeply misguided. This is not because these frameworks are invalid. Rather, it is because they do not belong in a field in which the formation of the object explicitly attempts to 'bracket' all particular perspectives in favor of an objectivity that would extend to any possible knower, regardless of her point of view. Whether and in what way such objectivity is possible is another matter.

We can extend this 'positivist' understanding of 'method' to 'human nature' as well. There is no aspect of human life that cannot be studied objectively, quantified and analyzed. And there are many occasions when it is useful to do so. But it is a mistake to think that the methodology of natural science is the only one appropriate for the study of human beings. In this case, we *are* what we are studying – the truth that we seek is not only a truth of knowing, it is a truth of being; and we seek it with our entire existence, with our passions, our emotions, our will, as much as with our cognitive faculties. Indeed, we know ourselves primarily through these non-cognitive (or at least 'non-logical,' because often contradictory) means.

Art, as Aristotle (1958) said, and as Pat Allen (1995) has reminded us, is a way of knowing. It is *poiesis*, knowing by making, as contrasted with *theoria*, knowing by observing, and *praxis*, knowing by taking action. This making is a forming, *Bildung* (the German term for formation or education), in the literal sense of the word: transformation into an image (*ein Bild*). Poetic knowledge proceeds by way of the imagination: we make forms embodying images that reveal the truth of what we see. This is not the literal truth of representation. Art does not represent, it makes present, and what it makes present, ultimately, is presence itself – the coming into being of the world.

To base our research in the arts means to engage the imagination in the forming of our concepts and in the carrying-out of the project itself. Not only may the initial inspiration come in the encounter with an image, but also the conduct of research may itself be imaginative. We must have faith that the imagination can in-form us, that art is not non-cognitive, but that it binds together both feeling and form in a way that can reveal truth.

The example of Nietzsche may hold a key. It is not only that Nietzsche is able to conceive of two fundamental principles of existence and hold them together in his thinking; more importantly, he does so by means of the imagination itself. By naming 'Apollo' and 'Dionysos,' instead of saying 'science' and 'art,' he marries image and thought, the aesthetic and the rational. Unlike Plato, however, he does so within a framework in which both terms of the opposition are accounted for. This is imaginative, passionate thinking – a model, I believe, for our work.

Let me note in passing that much of what has been called 'post-modern' thinking similarly embodies such an imaginative dimension. In the wake of world-wide technological destruction, the naive faith in natural science and the natural-scientific method has been challenged by a more imaginative conception of knowing, one that is often expressed in the style of the works themselves. This tendency is found also in different scientific fields: the methods of natural science, in their positivistic conception, are no longer taken for granted, and more imaginative approaches have come to the fore.

In a sense, the whole debate about methodology is a reprise of the *Methodenstreit* (struggle of methods), the conflict between the *Naturwissenschaften* and the *Geisteswissenschaften* ('natural sciences' and 'human sciences') that took place in Germany in the nineteenth century. Only a naive positivism would assume that the conditions of experimental research carried out in the laboratories of physicists could be reproduced in the study of human behavior and cultural life. Wilhelm Dilthey (1976), for example, saw clearly the need for a psychology based on understanding meaning, rather than one that looked solely at the explanation of causes (*Verstehen* as opposed to *Erklärung*), though Dilthey's conception of psychological understanding was based on an assumption of empathic identification that neglected the otherness of the phenomenon being studied – the way, as Gadamer (2004) has pointed out, that the phenomenon questions us as much as we question it.

What is different about the current historical context of this debate, however, is that the very concept of method has come into question in the sciences themselves. Action-research, participant observation, hermeneutic inquiry, constructivism, post-modernism, narrative understanding – all demand that we put into question the taken-for-granted distinction between subject and object that underlies much philosophy of science (if not science itself). When we carry out research in the human sciences, we are involved in what we study; we affect it by our research; it is not neutral stuff that we can survey from an Olympian distance without changing its appearance, as the object of natural science is usually thought to be. In a way, all research in the human sciences follows Heisenberg's principle of uncertainty. It is not that we cannot know anything and must have recourse to mystical intuition or ancient wisdom; rather, we must recognize that our questions affect the answers we receive. As soon as we research a cultural phenomenon, we affect the way it appears – it appears the way it does only because we view it from a certain perspective. If we change the perspective, we will change what we see.

In that sense, research in the human sciences is a creative act. That there is no pure objectivity here is not a counsel of despair; instead, it opens up the possibility that we can do research in a way that matters to us, that is passionate, imaginative and dynamic. We must free ourselves from a conception of research that is devoid of energy and life – such research will be of no interest to anyone, least of all to ourselves ('rats and stats,' we used to call such work in psychology).

Moreover, if we affect what we see, it is also true that what we see affects us. In our research work, we are working upon ourselves as well. If this formulation seems strange, consider historical research as an example. When we study the Holocaust, there is no neutral, objective position from which the phenomenon would appear as if we were not looking at it. The questions we ask, the matters that concern us that gave rise to these questions, what we count as evidence, these all depend on the point of view we assume towards this historical event. Works as diverse as Hannah Arendt's (1992) research into the compliance of the Jewish councils with Nazi terror, on the one hand, and Daniel Goldhagen's (1996) investigation of the extent to which ordinary Germans supported the extermination of the Jews, on the other, obviously stem from different perspectives. Yet each, perhaps, reveals a different aspect of the phenomenon in question.

Not only does the phenomenon look different, but also we ourselves appear in a new light after these works. I remember reading *Eichmann in Jerusalem* and being almost physically struck by what Arendt's point of view revealed (whether it was one-sided is another question) – from then on, I could only see myself differently. The same must be true for Goldhagen's work when read by a German reader (and perhaps by a Jewish one as well, German or not). Research that is worth doing not only changes the way we see the other, but also changes the way we see ourselves. It is a way of 'soul-making,' to use Hillman's (1975) term.

I would like to conclude by discussing a theatrical work I saw in London a few years ago, Michael Frayn's *Copenhagen* (2002). In this piece, Frayn recalls the visit of Werner Heisenberg to Niels Bohr in Copenhagen, during the Second World War. At that time Denmark was occupied by the Nazis. Heisenberg, a German atomic physicist still engaged in research under the Hitler regime, took a surprise trip to see his former mentor, Bohr, who abhorred the Nazi regime and was himself in danger due to his partially Jewish ancestry. What was the purpose of this trip? Was Heisenberg trying to help Bohr, to warn him in some way? Was it a purely personal visit, conducted out of sentimental and perhaps self-justifying motives? Was Heisenberg proposing that Bohr work with him on atomic research that could lead to the construction of a bomb or, alternatively, telling Bohr that he had deliberately sabotaged the possibility of such research in Germany? No one knows for certain – the motivation for the trip remains unclear.

Moreover, and this is the genius of Frayn's piece, the uncertainty of Heisenberg's motivation and of the nature of his encounter with Bohr mirrors the uncertainty principle of Heisenberg's research into sub-atomic particles. And the relationship between the two scientists also embodies Bohr's notion of complementarity. The dramatic situation thus imitates the scientific one; we could say that this is a mimetic conception of theater. *Copenhagen* is an artistic presentation of scientific theory; its theatrical structure provides an image of some of the most complex scientific principles that we know.

Moreover, this parallel structure extends to the staging of the piece, not just its characterization. In the production I saw, the characters move around a circular, slanted stage, relating to each other (and to Bohr's wife, a witness to the scene) as if they themselves were sub-atomic particles. Each of them exists only in relation to the movement of the other (Bohr's complementarity principle) – their bodies are in a dynamic relationship, shifting position as they speak. And the spectator shares in this dynamism and changing perspective. One section of the audience, of which I was fortunate to have been a member, was seated on stage, behind the protagonists. Not only did we see the action differently than we would from the 'normal' position of audience members, but also we were seen by the other spectators. Our reactions were fully visible to them; in that sense, we became part of the drama for them, as they did for us, since from our position we could see their reactions as well.

The effect was to involve us in the action in a way that made us question our own perspective. In fact, I had to ask myself, was it a good thing that atomic weapons were developed by the allies? Not, obviously, that I would have wished Hitler to have the bomb, but rather that I had to interrogate the price paid for scientific progress – Hiroshima, Nagasaki, and all the Hiroshimas and Nagasakis to come. Was Heisenberg a deluded, egocentric servant of the Third Reich or was he an inspired prophet of atomic catastrophe? Was Bohr an idealistic hero or a collaborator in mass destruction? What did I think about science and art? Was I like a character in Orwell's *Animal Farm* (1996), who might end up braying, 'Art good, science bad?' Or could I hold together these two fundamental perspectives on life without desperately seeking to resolve their contradictions? 'Art-based research' may be a contradiction in terms, but, as Jacques Derrida might have said, '*Vive la différance!*' This kind of research takes place in the liminal space of the imagination in which contradictions can co-exist. The poet John Keats once said that an artist needs the 'negative capability' (2005, p.60) of being able to live with uncertainty and contradiction without irritably searching for reasons. Perhaps then the reasons will come of their own accord. In trying to understand the essence of research in expressive arts therapy, let us use our negative capability of being open not only to scientific conception but also to artistic imagination. The result may produce not only a new conception of research but also a new vision of our lives.

# 11

# A Fragmented Totality?

## *An Interview*

*Jean Caron*: I thought I might start by asking you if you could describe for me how you view your current artistic or aesthetic preferences. Do you have a sense of how you could describe what your artistic preferences are, in terms of your personal attraction towards certain colors, shapes or patterns?

*Stephen K. Levine*: I'm not a visual artist, nor am I particularly oriented towards visual art. It's certainly something that I have an interest in, but the modalities that I primarily work with are theater and poetry. One of the problems with modern or 'modernist' aesthetics is that it tends to be based on the study of visual art; that skews it in the direction of privileging formal qualities based on the 'distance' between the observer and the observed.

*JC*: Then is your work one in which the artistic awareness is communicated primarily through words and movement?

*SL*: Not exactly. Let's take theater, for example; the kind that I am particularly interested in is theater that goes beyond text. In Western culture we can see a dominant emphasis on the word and the visual image. What's missing, first of all, is any consideration of the body and its experiences. I'm personally very interested in what has been called 'physical theater,' and I've done a great deal of training and performing in it.

There are two traditions of physical theater. The first is a kind of ritual theater, or at least a theater that has its roots in ritual. This comes out of the work of Antonin Artaud, Jerzy Grotowski, Peter Brook and others; it tends toward an emphasis upon ritual action, sound and image (in the sense of a tableau) and only secondarily moves towards the production of a text. But I'm also interested in another kind of physical theater, stemming more from the comedic tradition, forms such as *commedia dell'arte*, clown and bouffon. To some extent the two kinds of physical theater correspond to the classical distinction between tragedy and comedy. In both traditions, there's a strong emphasis on the body of the performer and the bodily experience of the 'viewer' (if I can still use that word, with its emphasis on visual experience). The viewer is not distanced from the action but is drawn into the field. In this way he or she is involved and challenged and is called upon to respond. In traditional aesthetics there's an emphasis on the 'disinterestedness' of the viewer and a corresponding emphasis on the notion of aesthetic distance. I think that that is a valuable notion, in so far as it emphasizes the way in which the audience member is asked to step out of his or her ordinary reality and everyday concerns. At the same time the concept needs to be put into relationship with the participation and involvement that the experience of art brings. This is especially true from a therapeutic perspective: we want art in therapy that draws people in, affects them, and does not leave them outside looking on. In fact, I see this notion of a disinterested aesthetics – in which one can appreciate the formal qualities of a work without being affected by it – as based on a duality between subject and object, a duality that has been challenged not only by contemporary philosophy but also by the development of contemporary culture itself. In any case, the traditional aesthetic framework does not seem to me to be adequate for the practice of expressive arts therapy. We need to develop new perspectives.

The other thing that's important to remember is that the very concept of aesthetics as philosophy of art is based on the perception of the finished work, not on the process of making it. For that reason, among others, I tend to avoid the word 'aesthetics' and instead use the Greek word *poiesis*. The word refers to making in general and particularly to the making of the work of art. I like it not only because it brings us back to the perspective of the artist instead of the viewer but also because it situates art-making within the context of human experience as a whole. If the human being is essentially one who shapes or makes his or her world, then artistic making is only a specialized form of a basic existential possibility; it is not something separate from human existence in general. Rather, what art does is to show itself *as* something made, thus illuminating what we may call the basic 'poietic' capacity of the human creature.

Heidegger was the contemporary thinker who first brought back the concept of *poiesis* as a fundamental existential capacity of being human. For him, the act of *poiesis* does not only produce a work, it shapes a world. When a work affects us, it makes us see the world in a different light; we could say that it opens up the truth of the world, a truth that had previously been hidden from view. This act of uncovering is different from the traditional understanding of *mimesis* as a form of copying or reproducing what is already there. At the same time, it is not a creation out of nothing. What is uncovered must exist in what is already there as a genuine possibility of being; otherwise we run the risk of art taking us into a pure realm of fantasy or, in its political form, utopia.

*Poiesis*, by uncovering new possibilities, is a shaping of the world; it is, you could say, world-making. At the same time, the poietic act shapes the existence of the one who performs it; world-making is also self-making. We always understand ourselves within a world. To say this is to deviate from the Cartesian perspective, in which the subject is a separate being from the world in which it exists. In most psychological frameworks, this isolation or insularity of the subject is maintained. One of the things that happens in art-making is that we see how the work mediates between self and world; in so doing it shows us how much we are 'worldly' beings.

The act of *poiesis* in expressive arts therapy is one in which clients take themselves out of the passive or helpless state that they may experience in their lives and instead become actively involved in making their world, reshaping it, taking what's been given to them, the wounds they have suffered and the experiences they've had, and making them new (which, as Ezra Pound has said, is the essential responsibility of the artist). Through this process, clients gain a renewed sense of themselves as capable of acting upon the world. They become aware of their resources as well as their deficiencies, and they learn that even within a restricted framework (and art always operates within a restricted frame), there are possibilities of development.

At this point it is the therapist who has the responsibility of responding, who is in the position, let us say, of a responsible witness. The 'witness' in this process is not a mere observer or bystander, as the word might connote. Rather he is responsible in two senses. In the first place, his primary responsibility is to help shape the session so that the client herself has the experience of something that affects her, that touches, to use the phrase of Paolo Knill *et al.* (2005, p.82), her 'effective reality.' The therapist's role is not just to 'process' verbally what the client does but to intervene to make sure that the client has a 'poietic' experience, one in which she has a sense of her own formative powers.

This conception of the role of the therapist, by the way, differs from what many arts therapists have been taught: that it's the process that counts, not the product. In expressive arts therapy, we don't separate the process from the product; rather, the process of making a work is only fulfilled in the experience of being affected that the work brings with it. The emphasis on process is no doubt motivated by an attempt to make art-making a less frightening experience for the novice. But the alternative is not to go back to formal aesthetic criteria. Rather, the effectiveness of the work is measured solely by its impact on the maker. In that sense a work can be crude or 'poor' (to use a term from the fields of both theater and visual art); it could even be considered ugly from the point of view of its formal qualities (lacking a harmonious balance between its parts, containing jarring and contradictory elements, etc.). Just as Shaw inveighed against the 'well-made play,' (1928, p.217) we see the role of art in therapy as going beyond the criteria of traditional critical standards. The only thing that counts about a work is whether it works; the rest is unimportant.

A secondary meaning of the therapist's aesthetic responsibility, in addition to helping shape the session so that it is effective, has to do with her capacity to respond to what the client has made. Almost always, if the work touches the client (and this is the most important thing), it will have an impact on the therapist as well. This impact can lead to a new act of making, a poietic responding by the therapist in the form of word, image, gesture or some other medium. This kind of aesthetic response can only originate out of a genuine impulse that arises from the experience of the client's work, an impulse that gives rise to the need for a response. In this sense, the therapeutic relationship is an exchange of gifts, in which the work of the client is experienced by the therapist as an offering, something sacred that must be responded to in kind.

*JC*: I would like you to say more about the responsibility of witnessing that the creative act brings with it.

*SL*: The word 'witness' can be a powerful one. Originally it connotes a martyr, one who is willing to suffer in testifying to his faith. However, for the most part the ordinary usage of the term denotes an onlooker, one who sees what is happening but is not himself involved. To be a disinterested witness is to be in a privileged position in terms of a legal proceeding, for example. If we still wish to use the word in a therapeutic context, perhaps we should recall its original meaning. The therapist as witness then could be seen to 'testify' (in the sense in which the word is used in religious revival meetings), to bring forth in public the experience that has transformed him. If you like, we can speak of an 'active witness,' to distinguish the therapeutic meaning from the legal one. In any event, part of the therapist's responsibility in bearing witness is to give back what he has been given, not just to acknowledge it verbally but to show by a poietic act of his own the impact that the client's work has had on him. In this way we see that not only the client but also the therapist may have a transformative experience. Just as the parent is affected by the acts of the child, and in fact we might say is brought into being *as* a parent through the child, so the client brings the therapist into being. Therapy is an act of *poiesis*, in which both client and therapist are made anew.

*JC*: Can you say more about your notion of the ugly?

*SL*: I think the limitations of modern aesthetics are shown particularly in its concept of the beautiful. Within that tradition, inaugurated by Immanuel Kant at the end of the eighteenth century, the beautiful is equated with that which is perfect in form and which gives a sense of wholeness or completion. The experience we have in our own time, however, is that of a lack of wholeness. I keep going back to Yeats' words, 'the centre does not hold' and 'things fall apart.' What we need is to find ways to live in a decentered world, a world where the old certainties of home, family, community and nation no longer exist (if they ever did, except as ideologies). Instead, we are called upon to become capable of assuming different roles and to be able to engage in different relationships depending upon the context we find ourselves in, and also to be able to move, to migrate from place to place – whether 'place' is conceived in a physical sense or an emotional or intellectual one. In terms of classical aesthetics, you could say that we have transcended the opposition between the beautiful and the sublime. The beautiful is considered to be that sensible entity which corresponds to its concept; the sublime, on the other hand, is thought of as overflowing what is given to us through the senses. It is an intimation of that which lies beyond experience; it is incommensurable and cannot be grasped by the concept. One could say that today experience itself belongs to the category of the sublime; it can no longer be contained within measurable boundaries.

*JC*: Does it have an eternal or divine sense?

*SL*: It could have, but not in the sense of a New Age spirituality that promises peace and harmony. As Rilke said, 'Every angel is terrifying' (1984b, p.151). The sublime quality of experience gives us the terrible face of the divine; it is the tempest in which everything is torn apart. In this sense Hurricane Katrina can be considered an experience of the sublime, as can 9/11 (though not in Kant's sense, in which we recognize the fearfulness of the sublime without being afraid of it). For us the sublime may appear as the wrath of God. This is something that marked the twentieth century, with cataclysms such as the Shoah, nuclear destruction and our immense capacity for genocide – all of which are possibilities in this time as well.

One could even think of trauma as analogous to the sublime. Trauma seizes a person like a storm, it comes on her from the outside and turns her in another direction, leaving her disoriented. Trauma needs to be lived through; it can't be contained, because by definition it is that which breaks all containers. The question for us then becomes, what kind of art is adequate to the experience of trauma? To me, the answer is an art of the terrible, the grotesque, the ugly. If you look, for example, at the work of Francis Bacon, the British painter, you could say that his images are horrific; they show distorted bodies, bodies that look like meat hung up at the butcher's. There is no sense of bodily perfection, as there is in much classical art. And yet the work has an incredible impact on the viewer. Our task is to break down or deconstruct the idea of the beautiful. The problem with the opposition between the beautiful and the sublime is that it leaves the beautiful intact as essentially harmless. The sublime is relegated to a separate and exceptional place as the repository of that which is terrible or sacred. I would say on the contrary that today we can and do have an experience of what I would call 'terrible beauty,' a disproportion that affects us to the core. This kind of beauty is what we often find in the work of clients. There are of course also images of peace, harmony and wholeness that arise; but to be genuine they must emerge on the ground of the disharmonious, which is in fact the everyday reality of the client. I'm resistant to going too quickly to harmony; it seems to me too much of an empty dream. I think first you have to go through the storm to find the calm that comes in its aftermath.

*JC*: You used the word 'genuine' which, to me, rings with the beautiful as well.

*SL*: There is a sense in which the beautiful and the genuine or authentic can be brought together. The notion of the authentic itself is a contested one in contemporary thought; it has been criticized for relying on an essentialist definition of the human being, one that ultimately posits a presence beyond time. Still, I think there's something about the notion of the authentic that's valuable. If you think of it not as an inner self that is somehow divorced from the world in which we live (which gives rise to the idea that I must withdraw from the world in order to be authentically myself), but rather, as Heidegger put it, one's 'own-most possibility,' (1962, p.302) then the authentic can have an important meaning. Since we are beings in the world, we encounter others and the meaning they give to things as something given to us that we have not made. 'Authentic' here can mean not something 'inside' that I bring out and show to others but rather the way in which I respond to what the others have given me, the way I grasp it or shape it, the poietic manner in which I can be in the world. Authentic then means a laying out of the possibilities for being that are given to me, possibilities for me to be who I am or, let's say, who I am called to be. In this sense of the authentic, there is no essence that I have to go back to; there is only the possibility of an existence for me to reach toward. I am in the middle between what I have been and what I will be, and the way forward is never clear.

*JC*: Does what you are saying have anything to do with what Winnicott calls 'transitional experience?'

*SL*: Yes, and also with Victor Turner's concept of liminality (1995), of being 'betwixt and between,' not in a fixed state but to use Heidegger's (1982) term, 'on the way' (*unterwegs*) – between what I was and what I will be, between myself and the world or the other, always in-between. 'Being' becomes being in the middle or being in the midst of things. I can never stand outside of myself or of the world.

   This in-between space has no clear boundaries; it is, in that sense, chaotic. What is chaotic can neither be predicted nor controlled; both those capacities depend upon a distance from experience that is not possible if one is always 'in-between.' This kind of chaos can be experienced in different ways. One is in the form of free play; when Winnicott talks about being (2005, p.108), I think of it as a kind of free play.

*JC*: He calls it a 'restful place.'

*SL*: Yes, it can be restful and relaxing; but it can also be incredibly dynamic, leading to unexpected experiences of creativity. It's a place where I don't hold myself to a clearly defined identity, where I play with who I am, who I'm with and with the materials that are there for me. To experience chaos in this way can lead to great joy. However, there is another kind of chaotic experience, where what Winnicott calls 'impingement' (1990, p.17) takes place. When there's too much 'impingement,' you have the experience of trauma; the world breaks into you in such a way that you cannot hold it; rather you are broken by it. This kind of chaos is extremely painful and difficult to deal with. What is necessary in the therapeutic relationship is to build a framework that can contain the destructive, chaotic experiences that bring the person to ask for help in the first place and to find a way to allow them to transform into the experience of free play. I sometimes refer to this process as 'playing among the ruins.' I think of it in general terms as a necessity for our culture, which in some ways lives in the ruins of the past; but I also think of it in terms of any individual in relation to his or her past. Who I am can often be understood in terms of what's broken down in me, what ruins have been left for me to play with and to use to build something new. Collage has been called the art-form of the twentieth century. Something about that rings true for me, in the sense of a putting together of fragments of experience, building something out of them which cannot be considered a whole in the classical sense but which nevertheless exhibits a logic of its own, one which I call a 'fragmented totality.'

*JC*: In a sense a wholeness because it's a totality.

*SL*: Yes, but not wholeness in the sense in which we ordinarily think of it. That refers more to the notion of a harmonious or completed whole, like Jung's image of the mandala in which the self and the world are one. I don't think that that kind of wholeness has much bearing upon people's actual experiences, particularly their experiences in therapy and, in general, in the historical epoch of which we are all part. It's easy for New Age approaches to lead people into images of wholeness that take them away from the world. Given a world of terror and mass destruction, what possible relevance can these images have? They have nothing to do with this world.

Of course on some level I, too, long for wholeness and I even rely on a faith that I cannot articulate; yet I am on guard against the false promises of both therapeutic and political ideologies. When I was first training as a psychotherapist in the 1970s, I remember we used to joke that above the entrance to the therapeutic space should be inscribed the words that framed Dante's Hell: 'Abandon hope all ye who enter here.' I still believe this: we need to give up the hope of salvation in any form. And yet of course I must believe in some form of hope or else I would not be involved in this field. Perhaps I would not *be* at all.

*JC*: What brings you into play? What are the ingredients that are present that draw you into the act of play, the act of stepping over the threshold and beginning to explore?

*SL*: I think I have to feel both a push and a pull, a push that comes from within, that originates in the sense that something is missing, that I have to go beyond where I am to find it. It's something about inhabiting a form that no longer fits, a sense that I've come to a stage in my life where I've outgrown whatever it may be, whether it's a relationship, a kind of behavior or a belief system. These don't fit anymore; they're experienced as painful or constricting, and there needs to be a certain de-structuring. This is the kind of process that goes on in therapy. To go into it, there has to be the sense that something needs to break down.

Of course, there also has to be a sense that there is something new that is trying to emerge, something that is calling out to be born. This is the pull that corresponds to the push. You don't need to know what it is; in fact, I think one can't know what it is until it emerges. The future is always a surprise. But there does have to be a sense that the therapeutic space is a place for exploration, that I can relax into it and let go of my customary defenses against the new. For this to happen, the therapist must create a safe space. Safety and trust are the basis of the therapeutic relationship, perhaps of any relationship. If you don't feel safe, you can't let go.

At the same time, we have seen in recent years a strong emphasis upon safety in the therapeutic context. It sometimes seems as if safety has become an end in itself, when actually the purpose of creating safety is to enable people to take risks. Safety is only the first stage of a therapeutic process; a constant preoccupation with safety seems to me to be counter-productive. I find that particularly therapists-in-training will often resist a process, saying 'I don't feel safe.' They seem hyper-sensitized to the issue of safety. What's interesting is that if you were to take these same people and put them into a different framework, for example a theater workshop, you would see them do amazing things and never ask whether it is safe. There's something about therapy today that overemphasizes safety. This has a lot to do with the framework of victimization and abuse that dominates the field. I'd like to talk more about that, but first let me go back to the theme of play. I said that a person needs to feel safe so that she can go into the play. But once in the play, I think she has to feel she can really let go, that she can be wild or chaotic, crazy even, and that within certain limits she can do almost anything. I've had experiences where I've seen people do amazingly crazy and wonderful things, things that I could in no way have predicted or forced to come about.

*JC*: As a therapist, when you're in this place of play, is artistic judgment any part of your decision-making, either in terms of an intervention or a response?

*SL*: This raises an issue I've been thinking a lot about lately, the relationship between play and art. In a way, I tend to think of expressive arts therapy as play-based; I put a lot of emphasis of improvisatory impulses, on spontaneity and invention in play. A lot of my own work both in theater and in therapy is rooted in that. At the same time I've been very much affected by Paolo Knill's emphasis on a 'work-oriented' approach to expressive arts therapy, one that sees the making of a work of art as the culmination of the process of creativity (Knill *et al.* 2005, p.110). If we take seriously the idea that as arts therapists we stand within the traditions of the disciplines of the arts, then we have to be concerned with works, since that is in fact what the artist aims for. The artist wants the work; she's not content just to enjoy the process. This shows the limitation of a process-oriented therapeutic framework. Instead, we want the work to emerge. That doesn't mean we go back to art school and the kinds of critical judgments that tend to be made there. Rather, what we want is the work that has, as I said, an 'effective reality' for the client, that has an impact on him, that moves or touches him and brings him to say, 'Yes!'

*JC*: Where does interpretation come in?

*SL*: It depends on what we mean by interpretation. In terms of a response based on a felt understanding of what is happening, you could think of our work as interpretation. But it is certainly not an interpretation in the traditional sense, as in classical psychoanalysis, an act in which the analyst is seen as standing outside of the experience she is interpreting. If you consider Heidegger's metaphor of the 'hermeneutic circle,' in which I am always involved in that which I am trying to understand, then interpretation means something quite different. It refers to an understanding from my particular point of view, not from the omniscient perspective of one who is 'outside,' but rather from the point of view of one who is in the transitional space with another. If I am there with you, I certainly have an understanding of what you're doing; I'm finding meaning or sense in it. Here I relate 'sense' back to the body, the senses. In French the word *sens* means both bodily sense and significance; it also means direction. The sense is the meaning that emerges from the body, from the gestural expression, and it is that which shows me where to go.

*JC*: This is interesting because the original Greek word from which 'aesthetics' is derived, *aisthesis*, means sense perception. And we seem to have lost that connection to the senses.

*SL*: I think it's also about making the connection between sensing in a bodily way and making sense in terms of understanding; it's important not to separate them.

*JC*: And that includes the imaginal. There's a bodily aspect to it and an imaginal one.

*SL*: Yes, the imaginal is important too. The whole question of how, to what extent is...the...I'm hesitating here because I think it's still not totally clear to me what the relationship is between sensing and imagining. There's a way in which we can talk about the whole framework of experience as an imaginal one (James Hillman seems to do that). We ordinarily think of sensing as primary, and imagining as based upon sensing. We think of what we imagine as something we have seen or could see, but which is absent. I can imagine my friend visiting next week, but I can do that only because

I have had or could have the sense experience of perceiving him or her. Although this is the obvious relationship between sensing and imagining, I wonder if in fact it's true. You could in fact say that sensing depends on imagining, rather than the other way around. Imagination is an understanding of possibility. In order for the capacity to sense to be possible, there has to be the imagination of a field in which certain things can be perceived. In that way you could say that imagination is more primary than sensing. Vision in the sense of the visionary comes before vision as literal sight.

*JC*: Isn't vision in that sense connected to what cannot be seen, what requires faith?

*SL*: This is an important topic for me, one that I go into in several different places in my writing. In an article in the book *Foundations of Expressive Arts Therapy*, I talk about the impossibility of relying on a pre-conceived notion of a foundation for our work (Levine 1999). One of the great achievements of contemporary thought has been to question the notion of a foundation or ground that we can rely on, one that would ultimately be rooted in a transcendent reality that goes beyond the historical world in which we live. Within this post-modern perspective, the arts therapies will have to find their foundation, if they can find one at all, in the very act of *poiesis* itself, in art-making as a way of responding to the joy and pain of the world. Ultimately there has to be the faith that art is adequate in its own right, that art-making is enough, not enough to substitute for life but enough to find a response to both joy and pain. I think this kind of faith is very important for the arts therapist. It also opens up to other questions about the relationship of aesthetics to ethics and to religious experience.

*JC*: We are scratching the surface of what for me will be a life-long exploration.

*SL*: For me as well. I don't think we will ever come to the end of it; the notion of a completed totality here as elsewhere is an illusion that must be given up. For Kant, only the vision of a completed totality enables us to keep going, both in science and in religion. Without the idea of the totality of knowledge, the pursuit of science would not be possible, and without the idea of a world in which virtue is ultimately rewarded, ethical behavior would be impossible. I question whether these kinds of ideas are what we need. I think what we need at this time of history is a vision that can hold the incompleteness of our experience as such.

*JC*: Vision and faith are close linked, aren't they? Faith implies hope in what is not seen; it communicates a sense of what is missing that we have not yet caught sight of.

*SL*: Perhaps, but the kind of faith that is meaningful for me is one that acknowledges that the gaps in our experience will never be filled and that nevertheless we can live with the holes. This implies that if we are to have a concept of the divine, it would have to be one in which the divine is involved in the world, not a perfect being outside of it.

I'd like to get back to the question of victimization at this point. I believe this has become the dominant figure in psychotherapy in recent years, and I think this is unfortunate. The problem, I believe, is not the emphasis on trauma that this implies; the problem is the lack of understanding that we are capable of being defined not only by the trauma, but also by what we make out of what has happened to us. To be vulnerable is to be human. We are wounded by our very humanity, in so far as we recognize that we will die. Whatever else that may come to shatter us is already present as a possibility in the very vulnerability of our existence. This is part of the human condition. But expressive arts therapy or any other form of therapy needs to understand that what is therapeutic is the capacity to respond to our wounds. In this way, we won't remain victims of the trauma. If you become defined as a survivor of abuse, you may not recognize that you are also the one who can respond to it, that you can define yourself not by your wound but by your capacity to respond. Students are often confused about that, and sometimes they have the sense that unless they can define themselves as victims of abuse they will have no right to practice as a therapist. I've often seen students searching desperately for signs of their own abuse, interpreting their dreams, for example, to demonstrate this. This takes away from the genuine experience of people who have been violated.

It also denies the very vulnerability of the human condition. Just being human is enough; we don't need to search for more signs of wounding than that. What's important is the way people can respond to the pain that they've suffered. If such a response is not possible, then therapy itself is not possible. If all we are is our pain, what can we do besides exhibit it? And even that would seem to have no effect within the framework of victimization.

Moreover, the exclusive emphasis on trauma takes away our capacity for joy, the other half of being human. We must find a way to acknowledge all the pain and suffering in the world and still say, 'Yes!' to our existence. Even if we are standing on uncertain ground, we need to be able to stand firm, to affirm existence itself, an existence that contains both the heights and the depths and that gives us the possibility of moving between them. In no way am I denying the horror of what we have done to one another. For me in particular the Shoah remains the archetypal experience of our time. I do not believe in a world without pain, without the suffering that the Buddha saw as intrinsic to existence and without the unnecessary pain that we cause one another by our violations. I think the dominant conception of trauma is based upon a vision of the human in which suffering is purely extrinsic, a phenomenon that is merely factual and that overlies the existence of a non-traumatized being. I would rather say that existence itself is a trauma. We are the beings who make a world out of the fragments of our brokenness. In so doing, we give the lie to trauma and refuse it the final word. Only the creative act, *poiesis*, takes us outside of being 'the ones who are done to.' How can we make something out of what's been made of us? This is the basic question and one that leads us to the fundamental human capacity to respond to history through the creative act.

Part III

# *Poiesis* after
# Post-Modernism

# 12

# Poiesis and Praxis

## Between Art and Action

What is the relationship between making and doing, between art and political action? Pierre Aubenque has written a provocative article in which he suggests that *poiesis* and *praxis* belong to separate realms that should not be conflated (Aubenque 2006). Aubenque follows Hannah Arendt in her critique of the concept of *poiesis* (making or production) as the dominant model for *praxis* (action) in the modern world (Arendt 1958). As Aubenque notes, Arendt understands *poiesis* 'in the Greek sense,' as the 'production of a work external to an agent,' a work which 'imitates a model considered good or beautiful' (Aubenque 2006, pp.40–41). *Poiesis*, conceived in this manner, becomes the basis for the technical control of nature; it is a form of instrumental reason, the shaping of matter according to a pre-existing idea.

Arendt's understanding of *poiesis* as technical control leads her to reject this concept as a basis for action in favor of a renewed notion of *praxis*, conceived of as action in the public sphere that aims to bring about the common good. Without going further into Arendt's concept of action (which itself might be said to have a poietic component in so far as she conceives of action as necessarily showing itself publicly, i.e., as expressive), one could ask whether her critique of *poiesis*, taken over by Aubenque and others, is justified. Arendt's understanding of the modern assimilation of action to the technical control of nature follows that of her teacher, Heidegger, who conceived of modernity as constituted by the activity of 'enframing' (*Gestell*), the construction of the world as material at the disposition of a sovereign subject. The disastrous consequences of unrestrained technological development have certainly justified Heidegger's critique.

However, Heidegger does not identify this activity of enframing with that of *poiesis*. Rather, he sees *poiesis* 'in the Greek sense' as the philosophical covering-over of a more original signification, which he tries to bring to light through phenomenological investigation. *Poiesis* as 'production according to a model' is indeed the way in which Plato and Aristotle conceived of it, but this conception is already permeated by a thinking of Being dominated by the idea of intelligible form. *Poiesis* within the framework of this thinking of Being can only be judged to be a poor substitute for theoretical knowledge. For Plato, *theoria* grasps the form itself; *poiesis*, understood as imitation (*mimesis*) of the things given to us by the senses, can offer only a second-hand and deceptive way of knowing. It is for this among other reasons that Plato exiles the poets from the just city: *poiesis* stands in opposition to truth, and justice can only be brought about when the city is ruled by those who know what is truly best for it.

Aristotle follows Plato in his conception of *poiesis* as imitation, but since his notion of form is an embodied one, he is able to account for the relative value of poetic knowledge as capable of bringing about a purification (*catharsis*) of human emotions. The poet, one might say, is brought back into the city, but only for the tragic performances at the festivals.

When it comes to true knowledge or to the right conduct of public affairs, in Aristotle's view, *poiesis* can be of no service.

One could ask whether *poiesis* 'in the Greek sense' is really the Greek sense or is rather the Greek *philosophical* sense. It is certainly not the sense of the Greek poets themselves, the tragedians and comedians whose work was celebrated at festivals which had both political and religious significance. The 'ancient quarrel between poetry and philosophy' of which Plato speaks is not conducted fairly if the definition of poetry (in the sense of art-making in general) is determined by the philosophers according to a thinking of Being in which *poiesis* has no place. Perhaps it would take what Nietzsche (1967) called a 'music-practicing Socrates' to provide a perspective that would do justice to the claims of art.

Heidegger does not proceed according to this route, however, but rather by a deconstruction of the Greek conception of Being, in which he shows that the origins of Western philosophy lie in the attempt to know and to control whatever exists. In this sense, the technological world-view of today is not a deviation from classical philosophy but a development of it. What is covered over in this development?

For Heidegger, the answer lies in an attempt to grasp *poiesis* itself, not as the philosophers have conceived of it and not even as the poets themselves have, but as the phenomenon shows itself to us. Already in *Being and Time*, Heidegger had demonstrated that truth as correspondence to a pre-existing reality is secondary, dependent on a prior uncovering of that reality as opening itself up to us. Fundamentally, then, truth is the concealment of the possible. In 'The Origin of the Work of Art' (1975), Heidegger goes on to state that art-making, *poiesis*, is one of the fundamental ways in which truth comes to be. By engaging in a phenomenological interpretation of particular works, he shows that the work of art is a 'setting-into-work of truth.' The work reveals a world; it uncovers a horizon of Being that was previously unknown.

This setting forth of a world, however, is different from the enframing of technical production. As the work sets forth the world, it sets it back into the earth. The world is that dimension of openness in which things show themselves to us; the earth is the hidden source from which world manifests; it resists appearance and can be grasped only as that upon which the world is grounded. The philosophical tradition has thought the relation of world and earth as one of matter and form, but the thinking that proceeds in this way ultimately subjugates the earth to the will to power. For Heidegger, only a poetic thinking that engages in letting-be (*Gelassenheit*) can do justice to the phenomena themselves.

This is a very different concept of *poiesis* than that of technical production according to an intelligible model. It seems to me that Arendt's conception of *poiesis* is itself based on the technical model of thinking which she criticizes. *Poiesis* from a phenomenological point of view is not production by means of imitation of a pre-existing form. Rather, it is the discovery of what was previously not known, a process that requires a giving up of control rather than an imposition of the will.

One could ask whether, even if there were some truth in this different conception of *poiesis* that I have put forth, it would have any bearing on Aubenque's central question, 'What ought I do, what should we do?' Can *poiesis* be relevant to action? This is a difficult question that deserves greater consideration than I can provide here. However, I will make a few suggestions that might be developed further elsewhere. In the first place, what would *praxis* be without *poiesis*? As Emma Goldman is reputed to have said, 'If I can't dance, I don't want to be part of your revolution.' If action is lacking in the qualities of *poiesis*, its playful, imaginative dimension, it takes the form of a deadly seriousness that kills all spontaneity. The slogan of 1968, '*l'imagination au pouvoir*,' is still relevant. Without vision, it is said, the people perish. Even Kant, the great apostle of reason, saw what he called the 'productive imagination' as central to the functioning of the mind.

Poietic action, as we might call it, begins with the premise that we do not know and cannot control the outcomes of our acts. For that reason, we must respect the otherness that is presented to us, whether it is the otherness of other people or that of the earth itself. By opening ourselves to the truth of the other (to his or her 'face,' Levinas (1998) would say), we dislodge ourselves from our sovereign position as masters of the universe. We are willing to be surprised and overtaken by what we encounter. We accept responsibility for our acts – not in the sense that we can control their outcomes, but in the sense that we are able to respond to what is given to us. Our actions hearken to the call of the world; they are responses that seek to open space for what is coming, for the advent of a possible truth.

*Poiesis* is always possible, as I have remarked elsewhere (Levine 1999, p.31). I would add here that *poiesis* is the ground of possibility itself. *Poiesis* holds out the hope for a world in the making, for what Jacques Derrida called the 'democracy to come' (Derrida 2002, p.252). It contains Walter Benjamin's (1986, p.254) notion of a 'weak messianic claim': not that the Messiah will arrive but that it is always possible that he is on the way. In spite of all the horror and catastrophe of human history, *poiesis* reminds us of what Stendhal (and Marcuse after him) called the essence of art, that it brings beauty, 'the promise of happiness' (*la promesse de bonheur*) (Marcuse 1969, p.115).

Of course, *poiesis* in this sense is not the provenance of artists in particular. Rather it can be thought of as the basis of a different kind of action, a poetic politics that necessarily takes a democratic form, one based on participation rather than delegation to elected authorities. Participatory democracy is *poiesis* in action, an acting-in-common that accepts what has been given to us and seeks imaginative means of making something new from it. And perhaps the poets themselves will lead the way. In every anti-war and anti-globalization demonstration, the drummers, musicians and puppeteers embody the energy of the event, its *energeia* or capacity for action. The joyous sound of the music and our delight in the visual imagery reminds us of what we are fighting for: a world in which the possible can be made actual, in which happiness is not at odds with duty or necessity, in which celebration is the order of the day even as we listen and respond to the cries of others and mourn what has been lost.

*Poiesis* is possibility; it is the utopian hope that has its place, its *topos*, in the present, in what is presented to us. For *praxis* to come to life for us today, for us to be able to act politically, we must leave room for *poiesis*, for imagination, discovery, play, spontaneity, improvisation and – perhaps most of all – joy. Only then will we be able to act in a way that can adequately respond to the question that Pierre Aubenque properly poses, 'What ought I do, what should we do?'

13

# Be Like Jacques
## Mimesis *with a* Différance

What is our relation to our precursors? Or should I say, our 'proper' relation, the one that is 'appropriate?' How shall we appropriate those who have passed? Can we, should we, make them our own, our property – in this case, our intellectual property? And what of *their* intellectual property rights? Do they still have any? Did they ever?

Jacques Derrida is no longer with us. Or perhaps he is only now with *us*, no longer belonging, in whatever ambiguous sense, to himself. His spirit has departed. It has become what it was always meant to be, a specter, a ghost, *Geist*. Perhaps it remains as the spirit of the age, the ghostly, ghastly time in which we live.

But though his spirit may be gone, his body (of work) lives on. It has become, is becoming, petrified, a stone on which to build a new church: the fellowship of true Derrideans. Can we imagine anything more abhorrent to the spirit of this work? It will haunt us, if we do not take care to lay it to rest.

How can we pay homage to this man, this thinker? How can we repay the impossible gift we have received? What is the proper tribute that we owe? It seems that the correct trope is that of mourning. Derrida mourned many friends; now it is our turn to mourn him. But, as he has taught us, we must first ask, what does it mean to properly mourn?

Mourning is said to be a way of coming to terms with the past, of freeing ourselves from it. Proper mourning, then, would be a form of working through. Pathological mourning, on the other hand, is thought to consist of living in the past, holding on to it, as if 'Get over it!' were the essential maxim for life. This urge to free ourselves from what has gone before may be a temptation inherent in our existence; we are, or so we have been told, beings that project ourselves into the future. And even if this were an inherent tendency, there are certain epochs that particularly pride themselves on their radical novelty. Every so often, moreover, an event occurs which makes the past seem irrelevant. What happened to 'European civilization' after the Holocaust? On a lesser plane (or is it?), has 9/11 indeed meant the end of irony?

All attempts to mark such a new beginning, a New World, a New Man, however, show themselves to be repetitions of the past. We may destroy all the clocks in Paris, as the revolutionaries did, but time will still be measured by the beat of the drum and the fall of the tumbrel. The Old Adam can always be detected under the clothes of the New.

It seems that whether we will it or not, our relation to the past is a mimetic one, in which we repeat, knowingly or not, that which has gone before. Indeed, we could say that those who do not repeat the past are doomed to remember it, to ruminate obsessively on what is no more. *Mimesis* is inherent in the passage of time, despite our struggle to free ourselves from it; but perhaps we can begin to think *mimesis* differently, to deconstruct the concept and set it free.

To do that, we must go back to Plato, whose footnotes we are still writing. As we know, or think we do, Plato's thinking rests on a critique of *mimesis*. He is quite clear that for him the artist, in imitating the things of this world that are coming into being and passing away, is three times removed from true Being, the unchanging Forms which sensible things themselves imitate. The goal of philosophy, for Plato, is to pass beyond seeming to being, to move from the semblance of what is available to our senses and arrive at its source, which can be known only by pure thought. In this way, philosophy ends by abolishing itself; the dialectical passage of thinking terminates in a vision of what does not change. Philosophy as visionary presence of unchanging truth transcends *poiesis*, which is based on the *mimesis* of time.

Plato, then, is the exemplar of the metaphysics of presence, vainly trying to escape, as Nietzsche saw, from the passage of time. His critique of *mimesis* is part of this effort. *Mimesis* never coincides with itself; there will always be a gap between the original and what comes after. This gap or fissure separates the mimetic sign from its object and opens up the possibility of deviation. The Platonic animus against *mimesis* stems from the vain attempt to close the gap, to abolish difference and turn the same into the identical.

And yet, as is plain to any reader of the Platonic texts, Plato is himself the greatest (I am tempted to say the 'only') practitioner of *mimesis* of all the philosophers. In the first place, he is himself an imitator. His master Socrates is the model whom he follows faithfully, that is, whom he betrays continually. Plato writes nothing in his own name. All his writings claim to be a reproduction of actual discourses in which Socrates took part. To what extent his readers believed this is not clear, and even today it is impossible to say where Socrates ends and Plato begins. The division of the Dialogues into 'early' and 'late,' where 'early' means more true to the historical Socrates, is a mere scholarly convenience. We cannot clearly distinguish the original from the copy. Nor, for that matter, should we aim to. To make such a distinction would be to remain within the Platonic horizon in which the light of truth can be clearly separated from the shadow of error. Socrates and Plato, rather, are one – and therefore two. They are united by what separates them, which is, after all, the mimetic relation.

Moreover, the Platonic texts themselves are exemplars of *mimesis*. They reproduce (report, simulate, pretend to be) the actual conversations in which Socrates took part. Their mimetic form is not an accidental addendum to their logical essence; rather the form *is* the essence. The dialogue is the manner of being in which truth is attained, even if the truth itself can never be presented in a *dia-logos*, a discourse passing through time.

All the mimetic tricks against which Plato inveighs are constantly present in his own work: bad men are imitated, sophistical reasoning is depicted, emotional appeals are made, metaphors are employed, and the core of the Platonic doctrine is presented in allegorical form, ending in myth. What is going on here? How is it that the sworn enemy of *mimesis* is a master mimetician? It would be a mistake to rationalize this contradiction by attributing it to the hangover (itself a mimetic effect) of tradition, to see Plato as not having fully freed himself from the mythopoetic culture in which he is immersed. This view assumes the Platonic doctrine which itself must be called into question: the argument that since *poiesis* is founded on *mimesis*, philosophy must therefore liberate itself from myth in order to attain to truth.

Plato's work, rather, reveals the insistence of the mimetic. The latter will return, no matter how hard we try to banish it or its representative, the poet, from the well-ordered *polis*. For *mimesis* is the manner of time – the dream, or nightmare, from which we are eternally trying to escape.

We are always 'post-,' and that means we will always be 'pre-' as well; the one depends on the other.

How, then, shall we live mimetically? How shall we assume our place in the passing parade? Who do we follow and who precede? If we come after Derrida, as we may or perhaps must, what does this imply for our style of walking, for our 'step (not) beyond' (Blanchot 1992)? It is in some ways easier to be a footnote to Plato than to be a disciple of Derrida. How to follow one who proscribes identification? The imitation of Christ is clear; we too can suffer and die upon our own cross and hope for resurrection at the end. But, contra Gerard Manley Hopkins, this Jacques, 'Jack, joke...immortal diamond' bids us otherwise (Hopkins 2002, p.181). What is the proper, or perhaps improper, path for us to take?

One clue could lie in Derrida's relation to his own master, who is not Plato at the beginning of philosophy, but Heidegger at the end. How might his relation to Heidegger be like our relation to Derrida himself? We raise questions here whose scope goes beyond the confines of this chapter. Some things, though, seem clear. Derrida is neither a Heideggerean nor a critic of Heidegger, an anti-Heidegger. His thinking of *différance* as that which both separates and unites would preclude these exclusive – and therefore mutually implicated – alternatives. He cannot *be* Heidegger, a goal which so many of that thinker's followers seem to seek to attain, as if the proper mode of reading Heidegger were to become him. Derrida is not one of the faithful, who define themselves not only by what they affirm (the entire body of Heidegger's thought) but also by what they deny (the historical/political site of the Heideggerean project). Nor can he be an anti-Heidegger, one who believes Heidegger to be nothing but a Nazi sympathizer, whose thought is an apology for Fascist deeds.

Derrida, the Jew, comes after Heidegger, the German. Even Levinas, another Jewish philosopher influenced by Heidegger, tried to escape from this dilemma. How to follow the one who followed those who would annihilate you? What relationship to this tradition can we assume without denying ourselves, without annihilating ourselves?

The key to the Derridean *mimesis* lies in his thinking of *différance*. A close relative of Heidegger's 'ontological difference' (the difference between Being and beings), Derrida's thinking of *différance* prohibits any nostalgia for Being, the curse of the Heideggerean tradition. For Heidegger, in spite of all caution, all crossing-out or repeated admonitions, the ontological difference is ultimately the path to Being itself, to the concealing-revealing essence of manifestation. If not a *nostalgie pour la boue* (a wish to go back to the primal ooze), there is certainly the desire to return to an origin, an ever-present yet absent source. The consequences of this longing, this quest, are evident. If we can think Being (no matter in what way Heidegger distinguishes 'thinking' from 'philosophy'), then we can project a return of and to the origin, a receiving of what is to come from what has been. Heidegger's error (or 'errance,' his wandering) can be seen already in *Being and Time* (1962) – in the very distinction between what is authentic or 'proper' (*eigentlich*) and what is inauthentic or 'improper' (*uneigentlich*), what does not belong to my existence. Proper for Heidegger is the anticipatory resoluteness with which I face my own finitude, through which I assume the dread of non-being and choose to be who I am as having-been. Here already we can see the distinction between those who belong to Being and those who do not. We can also see the possibility of beginning again, of achieving a moment-of-vision in which our essence can be revealed. It is perhaps only a small step from what Adorno (2003) called the 'jargon of authenticity' to the notion of a people who are themselves proper, a *Volk* who can appropriate their own historical destiny and, by doing so, pass out of the forgetfulness of Being manifest in the reign of 'enframing' (*Gestell*) (Heidegger 2003, p.298).

Is there then a 'metaphysics of presence' in Heidegger's own thinking? This question beggars thought: by attempting to catch Heidegger in contradiction, we presume to demonstrate our own self-certainty, a presumption which must itself presuppose that capacity to clearly distinguish truth from error that Heidegger denied. Nevertheless, we cannot shirk from the responsibility of going beyond Heidegger (even at running the risk which Kierkegaard claimed stalked all those who tried to go beyond Descartes – that of not even rising to Descartes's level). Perhaps this is Derrida's own mimetic task, to repeat the thinking of his master differently, to find another path, another trail in the forest of thought.

*Différance* is not difference, not even the ontological difference; yet it is also not *not* this difference. Perhaps we can say that *différance* is a radicalization of the ontological difference that Heidegger places at the origin of his thinking. To think the ontological difference more radically would mean to go beyond the thinking of Being. What then would remain at the end of the day?

Clearly we cannot go back to the metaphysical tradition; we have already gone beyond it. But neither is it possible to leave behind either this tradition or its destruction – or deconstruction. Derrida's choice is to engage in the play of difference, to situate himself everywhere and nowhere. There is an incredible lightness in Derrida's thinking, a de-light in semblance, in seeming and re-sembling, in playfully taking apart and re-assembling. He is a god – or at least a *daimon* – playing dice with the texts of the world. There is none of the Teutonic profundity that haunts Heidegger's work; rather, Derrida's *esprit de jeu* keeps him from sinking into the mud of Being, from being filled with the nausea which overtakes us when we contemplate historical time.

Derrida's *mimesis* is, in the end, a joyful wisdom. His serious play lightens up the world and gives us hope. The democracy-to-come is not the founding act of an historical people. The coming democracy is a multiplicity rather than a multitude, an inmixing of otherness, a chiasmic interlacing of both flesh and spirit which will finally take us away from the nation, the native, the people, all those entities which in postulating themselves simultaneously posit the necessity of denying the others, those who are different, who do not belong. Rather, it opens to us the possibility of a life lived across borders, not a choice between homeland security and alien invasion. There is always a stranger at the gate. Can we not make room for him at our table?

Perhaps Derrida is the first philosopher since Thales to don the mantle of the rootless cosmopolitan, the heir of all the wanderers, exiles, refugees – and not only the Jewish ones. He is both Odysseus, cunningly choosing to follow his destiny in uncharted waters, and Ahasuerus, doomed to wander eternally for taunting a god for loitering on the way to his death. He cannot be caught in immanence, but neither will he transcend the world. He is Hermes the thief, trickster, border-crosser, cattle-rustler, jester – a pied piper who gaily leads us away from home. For after all, there is no place like home.

In this age of renewed nationalisms, of renovated foundations, of fundamentalisms and creationisms, where once again the best lack all conviction, can we imitate this inimitable presence who is no longer here? What would it mean to be faithful to one who faithfully betrayed all? We must above all else, as I remarked before, resist the temptation to become Derrideans, to be franco-fiends and philologues, to demonstrate our 'mastery' of his texts, his sources, the tradition which we dimly comprehend. That would be a strange democracy indeed, one in which we would raise ourselves above the people by intellectual force.

Rather, we would follow our transatlantic benefactor best if we deviated from him by returning to our own fragile roots in the New World, our Whitmanesque embrace of all we encounter in the pathways of our non-native land. These days I see his ghost in the terrible angels of America, howling, naked and unafraid, against the winds of the imperial machine. I hear his voice in the scratching-over, the dubbing and re-dubbing, of the unheard sounds of the street. He was there when anti-globalization protestors catapulted teddy-bears over the wall of capital at the Summit of the Americas in Quebec City. All things 'counter, original, spare' (Hopkins 2002, p.133) mimic his uncanny voice. To remember Derrida is to be in-spired by him, to be in-spirited, to find con-spirators, to breathe easily together in the polluted air of our time. The best tribute we can pay would be not to mourn but to organize, to band together in our singular plurality. This *mimesis* would be the *différance* of the democracy-to-come. To appropriate Derrida would be to disseminate him, to throw him away like the singer who hurls himself into the crowd. We can carry his body until it passes out of sight and out of mind. His voice, echoing that same river into which we step again and again, will sing on.

# 14

# What Can I Say, Dear, After I Say I'm Sorry?

## Poiesis *after Post-Modernism*

After post-modernism? But didn't it just come upon the scene? How could it be gone already, before we could capture it with our gaze? Post-modernism could always only make a farewell appearance; the idea of a 'long run' is antagonistic to its style. Now you see it, now you don't – a vanishing phenomenon.

Post-modernism rejects the solidity of tradition as well as the revolutionary re-construction of the new. Modernism's Medusa stare, the fixity of abstraction, is no more a recourse than the 'in that time' (*in illo tempore)* of myth, the origin from which everything departs. Neither God nor Master – nor Master-Builder (the old foundations have not crumbled any faster than the new). Everything solid vanishes into air, even those renovated developments designed to house a humanity without illusions, a humanity whose clear consciousness of self would show its own empty core.

Modernism/nihilism – post-modernism/the overcoming of nihilism? But how, *pace* Nietzsche, could nihilism be overcome without a recourse to a new myth, even the myth of eternal return? And then what? By what effort of will could we believe in our own myth? Can there be a conscious myth, an understanding that what we believe in is only *Schein*, appearance or illusion? Would not such a knowing end by knowing itself, by destroying itself?

Nietzsche's heroic Overman (*Übermensch*), whose life is lived as art, making and destroying worlds, is the monster-god that haunts the modernist project. He claims the right to sweep away all that opposes his will, but from whence does the positing of the will arise? What must be swept away in order to arrive at such a positing, such a 'posing,' in the double sense of that word? Is Nietzsche a *poseur,* i.e., an actor, after all? Are we all Nietzscheans, players on the world stage? And does not this will to act end by abolishing the stage itself, as our play takes over the world?

After, always after, but what is the time of this 'after'? Does it ever become 'now'? In the post-modern revelation of the self-abolition of the now in its claim to presence, where does the 'after-the-now' situate itself – in a vanishing act, the shadow of what never appeared but only left a trace?

All right, let's get on with it – after post-modernism, what? After such knowledge, what forgiveness? After the after, is there a before? Still, we are born, we suffer, we die; the four noble truths endure. On what do we take a stand, what is our standpoint? Is it the still-point of the turning-wheel? Is there a faith at the center of all doubt, even the post-modern doubt of doubt?

And 'art,' can we say the word without putting it in inverted commas? Drawing a line through it? Covering it like Cristo? Does *poiesis* rescue art by returning it to its origin in Being? Can Heidegger's 'destruction' of art take us back/forward to the world-creating power of the creator-spirit, even with the knowledge that all creation is preservation as well? Is this after post-modernism *avant la lettre,* or a noble lie to get us through the day?

Who speaks? The poet and philosopher as 'unacknowledged legislators of the world' (Shelley 2007, p.75)? Says who? The Poet! Maker and destroyer of imaginary worlds – imaginary maker of worlds. And yet…the obligation to express even when there is nothing to express (Beckett 1969) – the obligation to express nothing. With empty hands, beginning in silence, listening, breathing, listening to the silence, the sound of one's breath, the sound of others breathing, moving around the room, around the world, hearing their cries, their laughter, surprising oneself by one's own speech, seeking, finding, losing what has been found, searching again, finding again, losing again, beginning again, ending again, arrival/departure, sauntering (going toward *la sainte terre,* the Holy Land).

Something is coming after post-modernism – after the last actor has left the stage, the audience has gone home, even the stage-hands have left. Something is coming to be born, some 'rough beast,' inarticulate, wanting to speak, finding words, finding song, the new *poiesis*, not bard, not maker, the new/old teller of tales, the rapper, hip/hopper, cross-over artist, klezmer, performance poet, bouffon, metal clown – after art and after the after-art, something irrepressible arrives, singing, wailing, shouting, crying, laughing – Caliban *redivivus*, Lucky articulate – she does not look back, he is not after anything ('after' = post and 'after' = end-gaming) – they are not angels of history looking back while being blown forward into the terrible future, they stand facing the wind, making music in the storm, going out into the streets banging pots and pans, announcing that the time for after is over, after has gone like what it came after, it did its job, cleared the stage, left space for what is coming. Now it has to depart.

Now is the time for *poiesis* to come again, for the *jouissance* of the play to begin, for Dionysos to be re-born. We forget what came before, though we remember it well. We turn our backs to it, knowing that history brought us here, to the place of new beginnings, but we turn our backs with a little farewell wave, we say goodbye to our friends and begin anew. Always beginning again, always hoping for salvation, for love, for redemption – yes, we know that, but we don't care, we begin again, we hope again, we love again, we play again, we are born again and we die again. Always being born, always dying, always 'astride of a grave,' we dance in front of the empty tomb, the dance of death, of life, of faith in what is coming after.

After the after is before, is perpetual being born, is 'birth to presence' (Nancy 1993), is coming into being and passing away – not the will to power but the will to play, to play in the ruins, to make collage out of the fragments, to differentiate ourselves from what brought us here, to praise in the midst of our lamentations, to sing *lhude* (loud, lewd) that *Sumer is icumen* in, the great noon-time that is after and before.

After we've said we're sorry, we can say we're glad – we drank from sorrow's springs and, refreshed, have turned our faces toward joy. Yes, after the catastrophe, after the burning, after the big one, we turn our faces to the sun and we sing.

This is *poiesis* after post-modernism – the new song that is barely audible in the wake of the great wave of historical time. Venus emerging from the ocean opens her arms and solicits our embrace. Together we can dance upon the shore. Together we can celebrate the feast. And when the fool delights in showing us our folly, we will delight in seeing our folly. And when the grave-digger shows us our grave, we will leap into it, both laughing and crying, remembering those who have gone before. In our beginning is our end – begin again.

Here Comes Everybody – let's begin again.

# References

Adorno, T. (1983) *Prisms.* Cambridge, MA: MIT Press.

Adorno, T. (2003) *The Jargon of Authenticity.* London: Routledge.

Agamben, G. (1999) *Remnants of Auschwitz: The Witness and the Archive.* New York, NY: Zone.

Allen, P. (1995) *Art is a Way of Knowing.* Boston, MA: Shambhala.

Antze, P. and Lambek, M. (1996) *Tense Past: Cultural Essays in Trauma and Memory.* London: Routledge.

Arendt, H. (1960) *The Human Condition.* Chicago, IL: The University of Chicago Press.

Arendt, H. (1992) *Eichmann in Jerusalem: A Report on the Banality of Evil.* London: Penguin.

Aristotle (1958) 'The Poetics.' In *On Poetry and Style*, trans. G.M.A. Grube. New York, NY: Bobbs Merrill.

Aristotle (1961) *Aristotle's Physics.* Lincoln, NE: University of Nebraska Press.

Arnheim, R. (1957) *Film as Art.* Berkeley, CA: University of California Press.

Arnheim, R. (1966) *Toward a Psychology of Art.* Berkeley, CA: University of California Press.

Arnheim, R. (1969) *Visual Thinking.* Berkeley, CA: University of California Press.

Arnheim, R. (1971) *Entropy and Art: An Essay on Disorder and Order.* Berkeley, CA: University of California Press.

Arnheim, R. (1974 [1954]) *Art and Visual Perception.* Berkeley, CA: University of California Press.

Arnheim, R. (1977) *The Dynamics of Architectural Form.* Berkeley, CA: University of California Press.

Arnheim, R. (1986) *New Essays on the Psychology of Art.* Berkeley, CA: University of California Press.

Arnheim, R. (1989) *Parables of Sunlight.* Berkeley, CA: University of California Press.

Arnheim, R. (1992) *To the Rescue of Art: Twenty-six Essays.* Berkeley, CA: University of California Press.

Aubenque, P. (2006) 'Kant and Aristotle: Two modes of thinking for praxis today.' *POIESIS: A Journal of the Arts and Communication 8*, 40–49.

Beckett, S. (1965) 'Three dialogues with Georges Duthuit.' In *Proust.* London: J. Calder.

Beckett, S. (1970) *Waiting for Godot.* New York, NY: Grove Press.

Beckley, B. and Shapiro, D. (2002) *Uncontrollable Beauty: Toward a New Aesthetics.* New York, NY: Allworth Press.

Benjamin, W. (1986) *Illuminations.* New York, NY: Schocken.

Blake, W. (1977a) 'Jerusalem.' In *The Complete Poems.* London: Penguin.

Blake, W. (1977b) 'Milton.' In *The Complete Poems.* London: Penguin.

Blanchot, M. (1992) *The Step Not Beyond.* Albany, NY: State University of New York Press.

Blanchot, M. (1995) *The Writing of the Disaster.* Lincoln, NE: University of Nebraska Press.

Borch-Jacobsen, M. (1993) *The Emotional Tie: Psychoanalysis, Mimesis, and Affect.* Stanford, CA: Stanford University Press.

Borch-Jacobsen, M. (1997) 'Basta Cosi!: Mikkel Borch-Jacobsen on Psychoanalysis and Philosophy': Interview by Chris Oakley. In T. Dufresne (ed.) *Returns of the 'French Freud': Freud, Lacan and Beyond.* London: Routledge.

Caruth, C. (1996) *Unclaimed Experience: Trauma, Narrative and History.* Baltimore, MD: Johns Hopkins University Press.

Conrad, J. (2001) *Heart of Darkness.* New York, NY: Dover.

Derrida, J. (1981) 'Plato's Pharmacy.' In *Disseminations.* Chicago, IL: The University of Chicago Press.

Derrida, J. (1997) *Of Grammatology.* Baltimore, MD: Johns Hopkins University Press.

Derrida, J. (2002) *Negotiations: Interventions and Interviews, 1971–2001.* Palo Alto, CA: Stanford University Press.

Dilthey, W. (1976) *Selected Writings,* ed. and trans. H.P. Rickman. Cambridge: Cambridge University Press.

Eberhart, H. (2002) 'Decentering with the Arts: A New Strategy in a New Professional Field.' In S.K. Levine (ed.) *Crossing Boundaries: Explorations in Therapy and the Arts.* Toronto: EGS Press.

Foucault, M. (2002) *The Archaeology of Knowledge.* London: Routledge.

Frayn, M. (2002) *Copenhagen.* New York, NY: Samuel French.

Freud, S. (1990) *Beyond the Pleasure Principle.* New York, NY: Norton.

Gadamer. G. (1977) *Philosophical Hermeneutics.* Berkley, CA: University of California Press.

Gadamer, H.-G. (2004 [1975) *Truth and Method.* London: Continuum.

Girard, R. (1977) *Violence and the Sacred.* Baltimore, MD: Johns Hopkins University Press.

Girard, R. (2003) *Things Hidden Since the Foundation of This World.* London: Continuum.

Goldhagen, D.J. (1996) *Hitler's Willing Executioners: Ordinary Germans and the Holocaust.* New York, NY: Vintage.

Hacking, I. (1996) 'Memory Sciences, Memory Politics.' In P. Antze and M. Lambek (eds) *Tense Past: Cultural Essays in Trauma and Memory.* London: Routledge.

Havelock, E. (1963) *Preface to Plato.* Boston, MA: Harvard University Press.

Hegel, G.W.F. (1977) *The Phenomenology of Spirit.* Oxford: Clarendon Press.

Hegel, G.W.F. (2008) *Lectures on Logic.* Bloomington, IN: Indiana University Press.

Heidegger, M. (1949) *Existence and Being.* Chicago, IL: Henry Regnery.

Heidegger, M. (1962) *Being and Time.* Oxford: Blackwell.

Heidegger, M. (1969 [1959]) *Discourse on Thinking.* New York, NY: Harper & Row.

Heidegger, M. (1971) *On the Way to Language.* New York, NY: Harper and Row.

Heidegger, M. (1975) 'The Origin of the Work of Art.' In *Poetry, Language, Thought.* New York, NY: Harper & Row.

Heidegger, M. (1982) *On the Way to Language.* New York, NY: Harper and Law.

Heidegger, M. (2003) 'The Question Concerning Technology.' In *Martin Heidegger: Philosophical and Political Writings.* London: Continuum.

Hillman, J. (1970) 'The Language of Psychology and the Speech of the Soul.' In *Eranos Jahrbuch 37.* Zurich: Rhein-Verlag.

Hillman, J. (1975) *Re-Visioning Psychology.* New York, NY: Harper & Row.

Hillman, J. (1996) *The Soul's Code: In Search of Character and Calling.* New York, NY: Random House.

Hillman, J. and Ventura, M. (1993) *We've Had a Hundred Years of Psychotherapy – and the World's Getting Worse*. San Francisco, CA: HarperSanFrancisco.

Hopkins, G. (2002) *The Major Works*. New York, NY: Oxford University Press.

Huizinga, J. (1971) *Homo Ludens: A Study of the Play-Element in Culture*. Boston, MA: Beacon Press.

Husserl, E. (1982) *Ideas Pertaining to a Pure Phenomenology and to a Phenomenological Philosophy*. New York, NY: Springer.

Husserl, E. (2001) *Analysis Concerning Passive and Active Synthesis: Lectures on Transcendental Logic*. Dordrecht: Kluwer Academic.

Jacoby, M. (1999) 'The Necessity of Form.' In S.K. Levine and E.G. Levine (eds) *Foundations of Expressive Arts Therapy: Theoretical and Clinical Perspectives*. London: Jessica Kingsley Publishers.

Jaspers, K. (1995) *The Philosophy of Existence*. Philadelphia, PA: University of Pennsylvania Press.

Joyce, J. (1998) *Ulysses*. Oxford: Oxford University Press.

Kant, I. (1987 [1790]) *Critique of Judgment*. Indianapolis, IN: Hackett.

Kant, I. (1996) *Critique of Pure Reason*. Indianapolis, IN: Hackett.

Keats, J. (2005) *Selected Letters of John Keats*. Cambridge, MA: Harvard University Press.

Kierkegaard, S. (1985) *Fear and Trembling*. London: Penguin.

Kierkegaard, S. (1987) *Either/Or. Part I*. Princeton, NJ: Princeton University Press.

Knill, P. (2004) *Minstrels of Soul: Intermodal Expressive Therapy*. Toronto: EGS Press.

Knill, P., Levine, E. and Levine S.K. (2005) *Principles and Practice of Expressive Arts Therapy: Towards a Therapeutic Aesthetics*. London: Jessica Kingsley Publishers.

Lacan, J. (1972) 'Of Structure as an Inmixing of an Otherness Prerequisite to any Subject Whatever.' In R. Macksey and E. Donato (eds) *The Structuralist Controversy*. Baltimore, MD: Johns Hopkins University Press.

Lacan, J. (1977a) 'The Mirror Stage as Formative of the Function of the I as Revealed in Psychoanalytic Experience.' In *Ecrits*. New York, NY: Norton.

Lacan, J. (1977b) 'Aggressivity in Psychoanalysis.' In *Ecrits*. New York, NY: Norton.

Lacoue-Labarthe, P. (1999) *Poetry as Experience*. Stanford, CA: Stanford University Press.

Laing, R.D. (2008 [1960]) *The Divided Self: An Existential Study in Sanity and Madness*. Ann Arbor, MI: University of Michigan Press.

Levin, M. (ed.) (1993) *Modernity and the Hegemony of Vision*. Berkeley, CA: University of California Press.

Levinas, E. (1998 [1947]) *Otherwise Than Being, Or, Beyond Essence*. Pittsburgh, PA: Duquesne University Press.

Levine, S.K. (1997) *Poiesis: The Language of Psychology and the Speech of the Soul*. London: Jessica Kingsley Publishers.

Levine, S.K. (1999) '*Poiesis* and Post-Modernism: The Search for a Foundation in Expressive Arts Therapy.' In S.K. Levine and E.G. Levine (eds) *Foundations of Expressive Arts Therapy: Theoretical and Clinical Perspectives*. London: Jessica Kingsley Publishers.

Leys, R. (2000) *Trauma: A Genealogy*. Chicago, IL: University of Chicago Press.

Lifton, R.J. (1993) *The Protean Self: Human Resilience in an Age of Fragmentation*. New York, NY: Basic Books.

Lukács, G. (1972) *History and Class Consciousness: Strokes in Marxist Dialects*. Cambridge, MA: MIT Press.

Lyotard, J.-F. (1993) *Libidinal Economy*. Bloomington, IN: Indiana University Press.

McNiff, S. (1981) *The Arts and Psychotherapy*. Springfield, IL: Charles C. Thomas.

McNiff, S. (1998) *Art-Based Research.* London: Jessica Kingsley Publishers.

Malinowski, B. (1984) *Argonauts of the Western Pacific.* Long Grove, IL: Waveland Press.

Marcuse, H. (1969) *Negations: Essays in Critical Theory.* Boston, MA: Beacon Press.

Marcuse, H. (2006) *One-Dimensional Man: Studies in the Ideology of Advanced Industrial Society.* London: Routledge.

Merleau-Ponty, M. (1964) *The Primacy of Perception: and other Essays on Phenomenological Psychology, the Philosophy of Art, History and Politics.* Evanston, IL: Northwestern University Press.

Merleau-Ponty, M. (2002) *Phenomenology of Perception.* London: Routledge.

Michelfelder, D. and Palmer, R. (eds) (1989) *Dialogue and Deconstruction: The Gadamer Derrida Encounter.* Albany, NY: State University of New York Press.

Mitchell, S. (1989) (ed. & trs.) *The Selected Poetry of Rainer Maria Rilke.* New York, NY: Vintage.

Nancy, J.-L. (1993) *The Birth to Presence.* Stanford, CA: Stanford University Press.

Nancy, J.-L. (1996) *The Muses.* Stanford, CA: Stanford University Press.

Nancy, J.-L. (1998) *The Sense of the World.* Minneapolis, MN: University of Minnesota Press.

Nancy, J.-L. (2000) *Being Singular Plural.* Stanford, CA: Stanford University Press.

Nietzsche, F. (1967) *The Birth of Tragedy.* New York, NY: Vintage.

Nietzsche, F. (1996) *On the Genealogy of Morals.* Oxford: Oxford University Press.

Nietzsche, F. (2003) *Thus Spoke Zarathustra.* London: Penguin.

Nietzsche, F. (2007) 'Homer's Contest.' In *On the Genealogy of Morality.* Cambridge: Cambridge University Press.

Olson, C., Mavd, R. (2001) *Selected Letters,* Berkeley, CA: University of California Press.

Orwell, G. (1990) *1984.* New York, NY: Signet.

Orwell, G. (1996) *Animal Farm: A Fairy Story.* New York, NY: Signet.

Plato (1987) *The Republic,* trans. D. Lee. London: Penguin.

Ricoeur, P. (1969) *The Symbolism of Evil.* Boston, MA: Beacon Press.

Rilke, R. (1984a) 'Archaic Torso of Apollo.' In S. Mitchell (ed. and trans.) *The Selected Poetry of Rainer Maria Rilke.* New York, NY: Vintage.

Rilke, R. (1984b) 'Duino Elegies.' In S. Mitchell (ed. and trans.) *The Selected Poetry of Rainer Maria Rilke.* New York, NY: Vintage.

Rilke, R. (1986) *The Sonnets of Orpheus.* New York, NY: Touchstone.

Rimbaud, A. (1975) *Lettres du Voyant* (13 et 15 Mai 1871) ed. by G. Shaeffer. Paris: Minard.

Ryle, G. (2002) *The Concept of Mind.* Chicago, IL: New University of Chicago Press.

Sacks, O. (1985) *The Man Who Mistook his Wife for a Hat.* New York, NY: Harper.

Sartre, J.-P. (2001) *Being and Nothingness: An Essay in Phenomenological Ontology.* New York, NY: Citadel Press.

Segal, C. (1997) *Dionysiac Poetics and Euripedes' Bacchae.* Princeton, NJ: Princeton University Press.

Shaw, G.B. (1913) *The Quintessence of Ibsenism.* New York, NY: Brentano's.

Shelley, P. (2007) *The Shelley Papers: Memoir of Percy Bysshe Shelley.* Oxford: Oxford University Press.

Tolstoy, L. (2007 [1869]) *War and Peace* (Penguin Classics). London: Penguin.

Turner, V. (1995) *The Ritual Process: Structure and Anti-Structure.* Piscataway, NJ: Aldine Transaction.

Van der Kolk, B.A. (1996) 'Trauma and Memory.' In B. Van der Kolk, A. McFarlane and L. Weisaeth *Traumatic Stress: The Effects of Overwhelming Experience on Mind, Body and Society.* New York, NY: Guilford Press.

Venturi, R. (1966) *Complexity and Contradiction in Architecture*. New York, NY: Museum of Modern Art.

Weber, M. (2003) *The Protestant Ethic and the Spirit of Capitalism*. Mineola, NY: Dover.

Winkler, J. and Zeitlin, F. (1990) *Nothing to Do with Dionysos? Athenian Drama in Its Social Context*. Princeton, NJ: Princeton University Press.

Winnicott, D.W. (1989) 'The Squiggle Game.' In *Psycho-analytic Explorations*. Boston, MA: Harvard University Press.

Winnicott, D.W. (1990) *The Family and Individual Development*. Abingdon: Routledge.

Winnicott, D.W. (2005 [1971]) *Playing and Reality*. Abingdon: Routledge.

Yeats, W.B. (2000) 'The Second Coming.' In *The Collected Poems of W. B. Yeats*. London: Wordsworth.

# Subject Index

# Author Index